The Thinking of the Master

The Thinking of the Master

Bataille between Hegel and Surrealism

PETER BÜRGER

Translated from the German and with an introduction by Richard Block

Northwestern

University Press

Evanston

Illinois

Northwestern University Press
Evanston, Illinois 60208-4210

Printed in the United States of America
10 9 8 7 6 5 4 3 2 1

ISBN 0-8101-1558-1 (cloth)
ISBN 0-8101-1899-8 (paper)

Library of Congress Cataloging-in-Publication Data

Bürger, Peter, 1936–
[Denken des Herrn. English]
The thinking of the master : Bataille between Hegel and surrealism / Peter Bürger ; translated from the German and with an introduction by Richard Block.
p. cm. — (Avant-garde and modernism studies)
Includes bibliographical references.
ISBN 0-8101-1558-1 (alk. paper)—ISBN 0-8101-1899-8 (pbk. : alk. paper)
1. Philosophy, Modern. I. Title. II. Series.
B793 .B7813 2002
190—dc21

2002001022

The paper used in this publication meets the minimum requirements of the American National Standard for Information Sciences—Permanence of Paper for Printed Library Materials, ANSI Z39.48-1984.

Contents

Translator's Introduction

In the letter that inaugurates Peter Bürger's inquiry into the fate of idleness or the useless negativity of the master (*negativité sans emploi*), he poses what seems to be a familiar question: What does it mean to think the aporia, to think the failure of language, without which, he tells his addressee, there can be no thoughts? Language is on vacation, absenting the very scene it has turned itself into. Yet this departure from itself by language is—and this is the aporia—the very condition of thought. In other words, language can only posture, mime its lack of essence now that its transcendental prop (*la butée transcendentale*) or its metaphysical stance has been removed. Gide taking notes as he travels down the Congo—or, rather, Barthes noting Gide taking notes—is the emblematic fate of the language of the master; it takes up residence elsewhere (*ailleurs*). Resistance or desistance, distancing itself from itself in the moment of its own self-presencing, is the disengagement from any project or productive undertaking that likens the works of all the figures Bürger presents in his text to the figure of the Hegelian master.

Bürger's gesture is striking for two reasons. First, it subjects aggressively anti-Hegelian thought to an inversion: Indifference (Blanchot's term, among others, for the contiguous existence of nonsublatable pairs) proves via that inversion to be formative, which means—and this is the second reason—it has a history, one coeval with the collective madness peculiar for Bürger to the twentieth century. Collective madness, if we are to take our cue from Bürger's analysis of Tournier's *The Ogre,* substitutes immediacy for mediation. The thinking of the master—and we will see subsequently why Bürger characterizes all of poststructuralist thought as such—is an ineluctable moment of resistance, be it in the form of death or fear of death, that renders all forms of (self) identity asymmetrical and contingent. This endless deferral of the dialectic is not only a motor of history (it is essential to the productive consciousness of the slave) but also history's stutter. Once we have discovered that the way of the world (*der Weltlauf*) is not as benign as Hegel assured us, but instead is as evil as it looked, this historical stutter might serve to realign time's joints. The historical character of the master's thinking lies in its mediating function, and this, in turn, is an antidote to the immediate forms of self-identity that Bürger associates with the collective madness of National Socialism. But if the idleness of the master serves to restart history, it does not restore history's utopian character, as Bürger notes, nor does it stall the machinery of the dialectic. Rather, the thinking of the master, a constellation that is the inversion of the productive consciousness of Hegel's slave, participates in and fuels the dialectic. It doubles and reproduces the aporia that prompts the delusionary appropriation of death or negativity by National Socialism. Finally, it perpetuates history by succumbing to it in the very moment it purports to circumvent or step outside history. Formulated as a series of questions: How does the gesture of nondialectical thought rescue history by endlessly frustrating it? How is the way of the world set right again? Can the aporia (of language, of history) be rendered productive without fostering collective madness?

Bürger's essay is less an answer to these questions than an attempt to stage the experience; in other words, an attempt to reenact as closely as possible the conditions for experience, rather than for literature and philosophy, that link the efforts of the surrealists with Blanchot, Foucault, and even Heidegger. The death of the subject or, at least, the subject's being unto death allows Bürger to think of that experience in terms of the Hegelian master. That is not an easy position to sustain. For one, the battle between two self-consciousnesses or the staking of one's own life never, in Hegel's terms at least, recalls Heidegger's own question of authenticity. For Hegel, it is rather a question of freedom, of "pure being for self" that, at first, can be won only through recognition demanded of the vanquished.[1] Being thrown into Dasein does not construct a horizon of finitude for the self, nor does "submergence in the expanse of life," to adopt a phrase of Hegel; rather, a battle with the other proves that there is "nothing in it [self-consciousness] which could not be regarded as a vanishing moment." Whatever name one wants to assign to the other,[2] the movement of Hegelian self-consciousness is distinguished from the others presented in this text by the desire for recognition.[3] A set of oppositions that only self-consciousness in its quest for being for self can display, in contrast to the relationship to Being or *autrui,* thus conditions the thinking of the master, which would seem to have little to do with the indifference of oppositions that was described earlier.[4] Moreover, it lends symmetry to a set of relations designed to instantiate the subject, rather than to destabilize it. It follows that without staging his own experience attuned to the resistance of another self-consciousness (and this is what all the figures in the text enable Bürger to do), he cannot rehearse Hegelian dialectics. The infinite interpretive act that since Nietzsche we have come to associate with all writing regrounds itself by substituting another self-consciousness for the resistance of the modern world. Bürger's characterization of all poststructuralist thought as the thinking of the master apparently hinges on this word "thinking," understood to mean something generated by consciousness of the existing order as that of an estranged self-consciousness. In the same breath, one is forced to admit that this experience has a Lacanian echo.[5] As Bürger demonstrates, the Lacanian notion of truth depends upon a construction of truth only as it emerges in the discourse of psychoanalysis. But it is the analyst, not the analysand, who wins recognition by mediating the discourse that results in the self-actualization of the analysand. The thinking of the master, one might argue, is destined to disappear into the imaginary like the image of wholeness from the mirror stage. If a single impulse can be said to determine the course of Bürger's Hegelian assault, it is this necessity to render for self-consciousness what is now its imaginary and what is seemingly unavailable to it as it begins to inhabit the symbolic order.

Hegel remarks how both the master's and the slave's consciousness are subject to inversions; the slave's consciousness is eventually transformed into a "truly independent consciousness" (*PS,* 117). That of the master's undergoes an inversion as well, since its freedom depends upon recognition by the slave; it is dependent upon something that, given this something's apparent inferior status, hardly fulfills the requirements for recognition. A certain groundlessness, not only in the form of death but also in the failure of the master to find sufficient ground in the recognition owed him by the slave in exchange for the latter's life, thus inherits the thinking of the master after all. Moreover, the master may know the work of the slave to be feckless, just as Bataille and the surrealists, for example, knew the futility of productive work, but he is dependent upon the futility of the slave's expenditure to savor the recognition that is really something less than the recognition sought. The only meaningful action for the master, as Bürger notes, would be something gargantuan, one that bursts through all boundaries. Death, in its configuration of the master/slave relationship, has already shown its meaningfulness for the productivity of the slave, which, however, turns out to be meaningless. The self of the master is thus necessarily dirempted. If for Bataille, the master is not so much dependent upon another (inferior) consciousness, it is dependent upon watching himself die, which, if the emphasis is placed on watching, means he cannot die but only simulate his death. His self-actualization is always incomplete. Therefore, the thinking of the master is "ungraspable," because it is only as such or as simulation. For Bürger, the structure of such consciousness echoes Hegelian dialectics clearly enough to merit its reinsertion in the very system such thinking sought to elide. One condition structures the gesture: The nonsublatable residing of differences next to each other, that is, their indifference, which in turn enables the dialectic. The consciousness of the slave, after all, is graspable. And for Kojève, the real interlocutor of French poststructuralism according to Bürger, it is the master—fear of the master, as Hegel remarks—to whom the eventual pure-being for self of the slave is indebted. If the way of the world were as Hegel described, then such a relationship would be the motor of history; it would account for the self-realization or self-manifestation of the proletariat. Certain is that the disappearance of the master from consciousness or from Hegel's text is essential to this history.

The meaninglessness of human endeavor (once the labor of the slave is viewed in terms of the evil way of the world) lends new meaning to the idleness of the master. The way of the world has to be inverted; its mechanism turned around. The simulated death of the master, or what we might call in less dramatic terms the shift between a construction of knowledge and its dissolution, halts the progression of the slave's liberation, which, as we know from Foucault, is a false promise that merely lures the slave to produce in service of a further entrenchment of power. The smile with which the master looks ironically upon the perverse labor of the slave is apparently all that remains for one who has seen the way of the world for what it actually is. For Bürger, this smile is no less than the playful assumption of a role always already awaiting the subject, even the master. In other words, the thinking or smile of the master is tied to the labor of the slave, who in his quest for recognition furthers the way of a world gone wrong. But in its being unto death, it also promotes the death or dissolution of the world. In other words, the master both enables and disables history, which, as stated earlier, makes him ungraspable. The history of that consciousness disappears from Hegel's *Phenomenology.* To make it visible, to bring it to consciousness, Bürger stages its experiences as a dialectic, a dialogue in the form of chapters, each of which is devoted to an encounter with one writer. This Hegelian gesture can be justified only by situating the groundlessness of non-Hegelian thought in a necessary moment of the master/slave dialectic, whose ineluctability offered the very mediation required for the slave's eventual being for self.

Bürger also seeks to justify that move by performing in some measure the construction of truth or, since its content shifts between construction and dissolution, its gesture. In the section devoted to Lacan, there is the attempt to stage a dialogue in the form of a letter addressed to Sigi. If the letter does not precisely mimic the construction of truth in the psychoanalytic discourse, the letter's decidedly monologic character is one of the results of applying Lacan to Lacan, something the writer of the letter expressly sets out to do. Such a move signals a consciousness of praxis. Rather than disable all truth claims, it seeks to rescue from the negativity of the dissolution of truth its inversion, useless negativity; or perhaps Bataille's description is more appropriate: Expenditure becomes productive. This point of indifference between construction and dissolution might be simply another attempt to name a moment of sublation that is as ungraspable as the thinking of the master, something akin to Blanchot's consciousness without a subject. One is tempted to call it a Hegelian sublime whereby the groundlessness of a consciousness without a subject serves as a condition for consciousness of the way of the world.

This, in turn, opens up to Bürger's very real political concerns or his attempt to discover in groundlessness a ground for the basis of an ethical judgment—or condemnation—of National Socialism. Blanchot's and Heidegger's political sympathies are a persistent preoccupation of the book, and a renewed confrontation with these same issues is the subject of Bürger's analysis of Tournier's *The Ogre* in light of Breton and surrealism.

What Bürger calls Heidegger's equivocity is central here. Drawing on Barbara Merker's analysis of the ambiguity of Heidegger's terminology in *Being and Time,* Bürger concludes that such terminological indifference is a characteristic of ontology or ontological analysis in which oppositions have not yet confronted each other as such. Being unto death, something Bürger links with the thinking of the master, is a suspension of the fear of death. A life that knows itself only in death, Bürger continues, is not confronted with the sets of oppositions necessary to make political decisions. Its stance toward the world is decidedly ambiguous; "the self lives in two places." Since only simulated death is experienced and thus, to speak with Barthes, simulated being, the issue is not so trite as to serve as a means to assault Heideggerian or even poststructuralist politics. Rather, it is a question of restoring authenticity to the thinking of the master, which now appears to be no less evil than the way of the world. If we recall how the thinking of the master is constitutive of the slave's productivity, the question can only be: Is history worthwhile? The hope for history, Bürger argues, seems to have gone out with the evacuation of the messianic from history, a notion Bürger obviously connects with Benjamin. National Socialism is inevitably the topic of this discourse since catastrophe, the messianic promise of history, proved to be as meaningless and inauthentic as the slave's labor. Hope is for the hopeless,[6] or hope resides, as Adorno remarks, in the possibility signaled by a falling star that this constellation might simply exhaust itself, that instead of sponsoring the dialectic, the thinking of the master might idle.[7]

A Note on the Translation

The original text was not always consistent in its presentation of citations from the French. In some instances, the French and a German translation of the French was offered; at other times, only the French was offered. Where only the French was offered, I have provided only an English translation. In the other instances, I have offered both the French and the English to correspond to the presentation of that material in the original. In most instances, English translations of the French are according to previously published translations as indicated. In some cases, however, no English was available, or Bürger's own translations were quirky enough to merit a deviation from what is available in English. Michael du Plessis helped me immensely with the French translations.

The Thinking of the Master

I. About the Essay

A Letter to Malte Fues

Dear Malte:

This letter is not a letter. The intention to publish it transforms the spontaneity of expression into the result of a calculation and the searching movement of thought into a rehearsed staging. Moreover, the form itself has an immense tradition: "The Letter to Leo Popper," with which the young Georg Lukács introduced his collection of essays, *Soul and Form.* What we term the spontaneity of linguistic expression, however, may only be an illusion; to be sure, one that we need. Perhaps it is not even a matter of finding a new form, but rather of making use of an already available one so that it becomes necessary or essential. So much is beyond doubt: More misleading perhaps than our unfounded trust in form is the demand to arrive at the issue, because in this instance "the issue" is not in the least an object (*Gegen-stand*).

We have often discussed the undoing of a literary science that has forgotten that foremost it produces texts, that language is not a transparent medium that renders content, but rather that language is the very "stuff" of our thoughts. We live and think always already in language. That should make every beginning easy, which nonetheless always proves to be infinitely difficult. The suspicion that with the first sentence the entire text might be determined certainly dramatizes the actual deed, but it recounts a writing experience that has caused many never to write down that first sentence.

If, in spite of this, we do write, knowing that the text will never be our text, it all depends upon making light of that knowledge, as if it did not concern us at all. Only in this manner could this letter, which is not a letter, finally become something, namely, an essay. Now the cards are on the table: There is no object to consider here; rather, the only issue that matters is writing.

That is anything but a license to indulge whim. On the contrary, the essay is a strict form. Its strictness is certainly not that of the deductive progression of argumentation but, more likely, that of a conversation in which each word has weight. The scientist follows a method; that is, he applies methods of analysis and an analysis of argumentative connections. He always has his goal firmly in view and will therefore always reach it. The essay, by contrast, is always threatened with failure. To be sure, the essayist is well versed in the methods of scientific argumentation and makes use of them, but the artificiality of those methods has become apparent to him. The methodical certainty with which reconstruction controls its own activity renders those methods questionable. He therefore seeks an antidote. Subjectivity, however, is also suspect; the essayist is concerned with a strictness that is not one of method. As such, he begins to observe himself as he writes; he notes how his concepts form an object and how that object is constructed by the indexes of his text. In this mode of mistrustful self-observation, his writing is altered. Strangely enough, it does not become more difficult (in that reflection, as it were, doubles the text) but rather simpler. The second reflection generates a second immediacy. Mistrusting the certain progression of his thinking, the one writing discovers therein gaps, breaches, but he abstains from closing them, hoping that such breaches will give rise to attempts by others and to other attempts. The history that derives from the essayist's doubts about scientific activity itself is obviously fictitious, but that does not mean it is untrue. Its deficiency consists in that it ties the essay to the essayist. That is the perspective of Georg Lukács around 1910. He could, however, distinguish the essay from the essayist, "who could behold the fateful [*Schicksalhafte*] in the form."[1] We can no longer formulate it as such. Unlike the young Lukács, our thinking is not poised between the poles of chaos and order, and it does not move toward systematicness. It does not seem probable that the completion of the philosophical system would announce itself in the subjectively postulated and, at the same time, necessary (symbolic) form. That is all very strange to us. And yet, the strange pathos of Lukács's texts moves us, because in those works he delivers himself to the movement of the text, because the author of these texts, despite his masterly gesture, is not master over that which he writes.

Adorno's *Essay as Form* (written from 1954 to 1958) also does not address our predicament, however conversant we might be with many of his formulations. Adorno draws out the consequences of a critique of philosophical system. His doubt about method leads him to develop a process whose goal it is to pronounce the particular without subordinating it to an identifying concept. To be sure, this process is performed without succumbing to the illusion that one could speak without mediation about this particular. As Adorno explains, "The essayist wants to use concepts to pry open the aspect of its object that cannot be accommodated by concepts."[2]

I know how much you treasure Adorno's essay about the essay, and it would be easy to cite those passages that appear to describe our experience: "The thinker does not actually think, but rather turns himself into a scene of intellectual experience."[3] Undoubtedly, that is *the* maxim of the essayist. But has Adorno himself followed it? Does he not always remain the antisystematic systematician? (In his debates with Benjamin, does he not always call him to order?) In short, does Adorno not simultaneously take possession of the essay and the system (even in the form of the latter's negation)? Even the *Essay as Form* seems to me to be shaped by this dual orientation: He describes a form (of thought), but at the same time he offers an exposé of Adorno's philosophy. His central motifs return in the introduction to *Negative Dialectics.*

Lukács constructs the essay as the form that registers a longing for philosophical system, Adorno, by contrast, as the form in which system survives as something that has been negated; to me the essay presents itself as a form that is no longer constructed with an eye toward philosophical system. That all sounds like a postmodern history of philosophy—and thus oblique. I mean in the first place something quite simple. Neither with Montaigne nor with Heine does the essay define itself from the standpoint of philosophical system. It ignores that. In equally small measure does it compete with the autonomous work of art or define itself in regard to its a priori form, the symbol. It positions itself between texts that it cites, comments upon, and tentatively relates to its own situation. At first, this positioning is rather unclear to the writer. He has repeatedly experienced the failure of attempting to go at the essay directly. The thought thus arises in him that a detour through the texts of the past might be the shortest path toward understanding his own time.

The essayist's intention is, of course, not entirely as modest as it has been portrayed here. He certainly trusts that his epoch and the form of the essay refer to each other—not in the sense of an absolute dismissal of system or of the "grand narrative," nor in the sense of a negative philosophy of history, but rather in a diagnosis of the time, which could be provisionally summarized by one sentence: The univocal triumph of capitalism is equivocal. In contrast to the famous Marxist dictum, it appears as if humanity poses itself problems that it is not in a position to overcome. But some form must still correspond to the total social aporia—not the paradox that merely affirms the aporia, but rather the essay. To be sure, the essay makes no such promises. It absolutely mistrusts "solutions." It harbors the suspicion that the facility with which we intellectuals would solve problems is more likely facileness. If certain predicaments are in fact inescapable, then the question arises: How do we deal with them? I do not mean the spectrum of reactions that stretches from Camus's spite to cynicism—those are visceral reactions that, however one may value them, all serve to still thinking. But how would a thinking look that posed for itself the aporia?

Any endeavor to recount the starting point of current efforts cannot escape the impossibility of rendering a true history—an impossibility demonstrated by Sartre. While contingent events successively befall the one subjected to experience, the narrator knows the starting point of that history and from that perspective lends the individual occurrence meaning. As a result, he misses the very experience he would reproduce. The following is valid in this instance as well: Whenever the individual essay reproduces its quest, that retrospective arrangement gives rise to the illusion that the essays were part of a project. In fact, the reverse is true: The project is a result of the essays. Only the essays reveal the aporia to which the essays appear to be subjected as a means of looking at the problem.

It is telling that the essay avoids being tied to a project formulated in advance. The structure of the essay is thus an experiential process, but in that process an inversion occurs. The constellation at the outset is transformed—if not into its opposite, at least into something different. What is decisive is that this transformation is not the result of the essayist's work on the object; rather, this transformation befalls him: "The thinker does not actually think, but rather makes himself into a scene of intellectual experience."[4] That is more difficult than Adorno's formula would lead one to believe. The self of the essay does not simply renounce its privilege to think. If the essayist is to make himself truly into a scene of intellectual experience, then he must outwit himself. That requires another's text to offer resistance to him. The stranger, the more repulsive the other text, the greater the chance he will experience it. The art of the essayist consists in making the other text so powerful that his own knowledge finally gives way.

To have an experience does not mean to step into a previously unanticipated fullness, but rather to bear the retreat of certainty. In our everyday existence, we take a number of precautions to protect us from having such an experience. In times of radical change, such security systems are destroyed from without. The essay mimes radical change. The measurement of its success is whether or not it produces an experience.

But how does one produce an experience? Do describable procedures exist for doing so? That none such exist nor can exist is easily stated, but that is hardly of any help in the matter. Experience, we said, should be a process of disillusionment (*Ent-täuschung*). Its object is our putative knowledge. The process is set in motion through the confrontation of our knowledge with the strange text. Even the process, however, does not simply express the truth; more likely, it contradicts itself (at least this is the assumption of the essayist). The essayist immerses himself in these contradictions; he does so not to expose them, but rather on the assumption that the truth shifts within them. The truth disillusions him; therefore, he defends himself against it. The essay does no more nor no less than manifest this struggle. Whereas the ideological critic knows that the truth unfolding in history is on his side and thereby finds a means to legitimate his judgment, the essayist exposes his thinking to an inversion, against which he can defend himself only insofar as he, for his part, inverts the inversion. The essay points to no exits unless such exits are immediately recognizable as paths that lead nowhere (*Holzwege*). The essay is the form of endless postponement. Its internal tense is the future, even when it speaks of something past. If the essayist has a process, then it is trust in that which lies distant. He hopes that an impetus or shock to reverse his knowledge will come out of this. In this respect, he shares with Benjamin the surrealist posture of expecting. . . .

This letter is no letter, but perhaps it has become an essay. Indeed, it disillusions. The current return of the essay, as has been demonstrated, does not have the historical necessity that I ascribed to it. Does the essay therefore always destroy the knowledge it produces? It appears, in any case, to be so today. Which, then again, is not so surprising given the state of the world. That our truth shifts between the construction of knowledge and its disillusioning dissolution is something, however, that the essayist stubbornly trusts.

Bremen
19 March 1990

2. To Think Madness

The Postmodern Novel, Surrealism, and Hegel

Since the beginning of the 1970s, National Socialism has enjoyed a cultural currency, which here in Germany has been rather vexing. In his book, Patrick Modiano draws a glittering portrait of the time of the German occupation in which cruelty and fascination blend. *The Ogre,* certainly the most important work to date by Michel Tournier, not only takes place in National Socialist Germany but also has as its protagonist a Frenchman, who searches for this Germany with his heart and soul. The poststructuralist philosophers Derrida and Lyotard see their task in the end to think National Socialism. Contact with this literature is difficult for us Germans. Either we run the risk of turning our irritation into a value judgment and impute to the authors an unconfessed fascination with fascism, or we seek to retreat to an apparent objectivity, which in the face of a matter that concerns us is hardly less questionable. As no manner of correct speech about fascism is available, so too is there none about the aforementioned French approaches to our most recent past. Since silence, however, would be the worst course, nothing else remains but nonetheless to speak. That should not occur from a position of unflinching judgment and critique or from specious partiality, but rather from the awareness that what would be the appropriate manner of speaking is to be produced first of all by writing. If between the decisionism of the critic and the objectivism of supposedly impartial representation a third path exists, which does not lead to caprice, it would be that of the essayist, who turns his ignorance, his refusal to pass binding judgments, into a formal principle.

Michel Tournier's *The Ogre* is a monstrous book.[1] The essayist exposes himself to it. That is not easy, since Tournier shows us the world from the perspective of a paranoid garage owner whose name, quite significantly, is Abel Tiffauges and for whom everything becomes a sign or an omen. As such, *The Ogre* reads as a novel of initiation. From his stay in the close quarters of a boys' boarding school through a brief war episode and up to his imprisonment in fascist Germany, Abel Tiffauges experiences life as a progressive advance into the mysteries that join his existence to the fate of the world. From an older schoolmate he learns to read the world as a universe of signs that refers to him. Reality confirms this mad hermeneutic. When he returns to school in expectation of draconian punishment, the school is enveloped in flames. . . . He experiences his internment during the war, which, among other things, bring him to East Prussian Rominten, Göring's hunting grounds, and to Napola Kaltenborn,[2] not as a constraint imposed upon him from the outside, but rather as a progressive revealing of his own self. Through children in the youth cults of National Socialism he rediscovers his calling, one that is not free of sadistic impulses. And it is only logical that shortly before the end of the war and during his final phase at Napola, it falls upon him to recruit the next generation of students for this elite Nazi school. Tiffauges, whose passion it is to carry children, is at once a friend and helper to children and, at the same time, the cannibal or ogre of fairy tales who robs parents of their children. The novel ends with the fall of Napola, which the fanatic director, along with the children, defends until the very end from the advance of the Russian army. Tiffauges, who flees the murderous battle with a Jewish child on his back, sinks—willingly/unwillingly—into a quagmire: The rescue of the Jewish child and the general collapse accompanying it coincide.

Aesthetic judgment frustrates any attempt to take the book seriously. Germany is seen as a transfer image, like the one French textbooks of the first half of the century could have dared to convey: the marshy East Prussian landscape and the wooded hunting grounds with elks and ten-pointer stags. German words and place-names resound in these parts like barbaric drums: Moorhof, l'Elchwald, and Pumpernickel. From a farmhouse window Tiffauges views Germany as idyllic:

L'un des petits carreaux encadrait exactement le bas du village de Wildhorst, ses maisons chaulées jusqu'aux fenêtres de l'etage, lambrissées ensuite jusqu'au toit, la mignonne église au clocher de bois, une boucle de chemin où il vit passer une vieille femme remorquant un bébé sur une luge, une fillette chassant du bout d'une badine un troupeau d'oies indignées, un traîneau de billes de sapins tiré par deux chevaux. (*RA*, 280)

One of the casements just framed the lower part of the village of Wildhorst, its houses whitewashed up to the first-floor windows, then paneled to the roof, the pretty church with its wooden steeple, a bit of road on which he could see an old woman pulling a baby along on a sled, a little girl chasing with a stick a flock of angry geese, a sled of pine logs drawn by two horses. (*TO*, 178–79)

And what is to be made of the depiction of the Third Reich's luminaries in which Göring appears as a moody big baby dependent on a fatherly "chief forester" to ration out the pleasures of the hunt to him? Since Göring is not permitted to shoot the ten-pointer, the forester prepares a wholly select pleasure for him: a bloodbath among stags, who, herded into a gully, have been cut off from all escape routes. The entire tale culminates in a theory that, reminiscent of the clichés of folk psychology, defines Germany "as the land of pure essences."

A l'opposé de la France, terre océanique, noyée de brumes, et aux lignes gommées par d'infinis dégradés, l'Allemagne continentale, plus dure et plus rudimentaire, était le pays du dessin appuyé, simplifié, stylisé, facilement lu et retenu. [. . .] Le facteur français tenait à rappeler toujours par un certain débraillé qu'il était aussi père de famille, électeur, joueur de pétanque. Au lieu que le facteur allemand, engoncé dans son bel uniforme, coïncidait sans bavure avec son personnage. (*RA*, 280)

Unlike the oceanic land of France, shrouded in mists, its lines blurred by receding shades, continental Germany, more harsh and rudimentary, was the country of strong, simplified, stylized drawings that were easily read and maintained. [. . .] The French postman always liked to remind people, by a certain unbuttoned look to his uniform, that he was also a father, a voter, and a bowling enthusiast. Whereas the German postman, bundled up in his smart uniform, exactly coincided with his role. (*TO*, 179)

With that, a judgment about the novel appears to have been pronounced: a series of clichés, which are then interpreted by a cliché-ridden theory. An intelligent author has expended a lot of energy to write a stupid book.

Objection: The negative aesthetic judgment could be an expression of (my) resistance. The book, in this case, would be talking about a subject I do not want to talk about. The suspicion demands that the interpretation be pursued. The portrait of Germany that connects everything with everything else should not be attributed to the author but rather to the character. Even those parts of the book in which the narrator rather than Tiffauges speaks are written from the perspective of the protagonist. The provocation consists in the fact that Tiffauges's paranoid perspective is never corrected within the novel but rather reinforced by the events of the novel and the philosophy of its other characters. The position of one who rejects the novel on aesthetic grounds approaches the opinion of the court that reproached Flaubert for not having presented a single moral role model by which other figures could have been critiqued. Aesthetic judgment arises as a defense against provocation.

The Inversion of Surrealism

Recognizing inherent defense mechanisms does not mean that their power has been defused. Only by successfully making the novel into an experience might that occur. Tournier himself urges the essayist in that direction insofar as he traces his hallucinatory realism back to the hyperrealism of surrealist painting. Where does one arrive when one follows this track and questions the nature of the friction between text and subtext?

In the last of the surrealist manifestos that Breton himself prepared, he included the late work *Du Surréalisme dans ses oeuvres vives.* In the conclusion of that piece, he considers once again the significance of the poetic image. For surrealism, it lies in the ability to connect disparate elements of reality through arcs of light:

> *Il [l'esprit] vérifie alors, fragmentairement il est vrai, du moins* par lui même, *que "tout ce qui est en haut est comme ce qui est en bas" et tout ce qui est dedans comme ce qui est en dehors. Le monde, à partir de là, s'offre à lui comme un cryptogramme qui ne demeure indéchiffrable qu'autant que l'on n'est pas rompu à la gymnastique acrobatique permettant à volonté de passer d'un agrès à l'autre.*[3]
>
> The mind then proves to itself, fragmentarily of course, but at least *by itself,* that "everything above is like everything below" and everything inside is like everything outside. The world thereupon seems to be like a cryptogram which remains indecipherable only so long as one is not

thoroughly familiar with the gymnastics that permit one to pass at will from one piece of apparatus to another. (*Eng.*, 302–3)

The world as cryptogram: The formula describes exactly the disposition of the Tournierian protagonist to the world. At the beginning of Tiffauges's journal, there is the following entry: "Tout est signe. Mais il faut une lumière ou un cri éclatants pour percer notre myopie ou notre surdité" (*RA*, 15) ("All is sign. But only a piercing light or shriek will penetrate our blunted sight and hearing"; *TO*, 5). In the course of the novel, the reader witnesses the manner in which the world for Tiffauges is revealed as an immanent universe of signs.

The child is of one of the figures through which surrealism seeks to capture an image of liberated existence. The first surrealist manifesto immediately evokes the freedom of childlike existence:

> *Chaque matin, des enfants partent sans inquiétude. Tout est près, les pires conditions matérielles sont excellentes. Les bois sont blancs ou noirs, on ne dormira jamais.* (*MS*, 12)

> Children set off each day without a worry in the world. Everything is near at hand, the worst material conditions are fine. The woods are white or black, one will never sleep. (*Eng.*, 3–4)

And a little later in the same text:

> *C'est peut-être l'enfance qui approche le plus de la "varie vie" [. . .] l'enfance où tout concourait cependant à la possession efficace, et sans aléas, de soi-même. Grâce au surréalisme, il semble que ces chances reviennent. C'est comme si l'on courait encore à son salut, ou à sa perte. On revit, dans l'ombre, une terreur précieuse.* (*MS*, 55)

> It is perhaps childhood that comes closest to one's "real life"; [. . .] childhood where everything nevertheless conspires to bring about the effective, risk-free possession of oneself. Thanks to Surrealism, it seems that opportunity knocks a second time. It is as though we were still running toward our salvation, or our perdition. In the shadow we again see a precious terror. (*Eng.*, 40)

Nestor, friend and protector of the small Abel Tiffauges at boarding school, has realized in his own way the surrealist project of returning to childhood, and the protagonist would like to follow him there.

One might continue enumerating the attitudes and motifs that link

Tournier's novel with surrealism. One might even trace Tiffauges's speculation about an androgynous Adam (*TO,* 17–18) to Breton's discourse about original androgyny (*MS,* 184). None of that, however, alters the fact that the relation between these two works is in the final analysis merely an apparent or inverted one. What certainly holds for the surrealists during the first decade of the movement is that surrealism does not want to produce literary works but rather to change life. Its rejection of the novel is relentless. Breton adopts Valéry's critique of the arbitrary quality of every novel's beginning and can only regard the novel's realistic description as a stringing together of clichés. Aragon is said to have destroyed a rather thick novel in the mid-1920s because he chanced upon the group's rejection of the novel.[4] By contrast, Tournier is, one might dare say, a novelist by conviction. Fiction is not a medium of which he might, for better or for worse, make use, but rather the necessary object of his literary activity. For him, it is about the plausibility of the implausible. The uncertainty that the surrealist seeks to arouse by renouncing the medium of fiction Tournier wants to achieve precisely with the help of fiction.

Breton does not want to write a novel with *Nadja.* "Who am I?" reads the first sentence of the book. In all seriousness, it is Breton. That is the reason for the pathos of authenticity as well as the elevated moral position of the writing self. Tournier, on the other hand, disappears almost entirely behind his protagonist. A moral subject cannot be discerned in his text.

In an altered framework, surrealist motifs also assume a different status. Unburdened by the demand to be starting points for liberation from self-imposed constraints, such motifs become elements of a game in the context of an admitted fiction. To a certain degree, one could say that Tournier has written a surrealist novel with *The Ogre.* Tiffauges lives entirely according to the laws of his own desire, save that the secret goal of that desire is not liberation but instead catastrophe. Tiffauges shares the surrealist privileging of childhood as the age of maximum intensity, but what he makes of it is the opposite of the surrealist dream of grand freedom, namely, sadistic repression and masochistic submission. Even the surrealist reading of the world as a universe of signs is systematically turned into its opposite by Tournier.

In Breton's *Nadja,* reality is interpreted as a world of signs, but certainly in a different sense from Tournier's. At the beginning of the text, which is based upon autobiographical material, Breton reports a series of events that, however insignificant they may appear to the reader, are tied for the author to a feeling that something essential depends upon them.

Il s'agit de faits qui, fussent-ils de l'ordre de la constatation pure, présentent chaque fois toutes les apparences d'un signal, sans qu'on puisse dire au juste de quel signal, qui font qu'en pleine solitude, je me découvre d'invraisemblables complicités, qui me convainquent de mon illusion toutes les fois que je me crois seul à la barre du navire.[5]

I am concerned, I say, with fact which may belong to the order of pure observation, but which, on each occasion present all the appearances of a signal, without our being able to say precisely which signal, and of what; facts which when I am alone permit me to enjoy unlikely complicities, which convince me of my error in occasionally presuming I stand at the helm alone.

Breton describes these occurrences as slope facts or cliff facts, because they rock the self's consciousness of reality by making apparent the presence of inconceivable connections and correspondences. An example: A young man approaches Breton at a theater performance; he has mistaken Breton for a friend missing at war. At a subsequent meeting with Paul Eluard, it turns out that he was the young man who had addressed Breton. Breton does not comment on the passage, but it is clear that he understands the peculiar meeting as a harbinger of a friendship with Eluard.

In retrospect, the sign acquires a singular meaning. That is in no way always the case for facts reported by Breton. Often it is only a question of a firmly held expectation that an object or a place could become meaningful for him. What is decisive for the surrealists is less the fulfillment than the expectation projected onto the object. In addition, the slope facts appear in isolation. They fragment the continuity of everyday existence but do not establish a connection among themselves. As such, they can be grasped as a manner to establish relations with life in the big city, as an effort to rediscover what is wondrous in a world shaped by science and technology.

It is not difficult to interpret the protagonist of a Tournier novel as a surrealist figure. He lives in expectation of a future happening, much like the surrealist, and disparate phenomena crystallize into structures of meaning for him as well. But what from the standpoint of surrealism is a punctuated event is developed into a system by Abel Tiffauges. Specific individual events do not have the character of a sign for Tiffauges, but rather the world consists only of signs, and these ultimately join his personal fate to that of the world. When he is threatened with trial for the rape of an underage girl, world war breaks out and the prosecutor waives the charge. Internment in National Socialist Germany becomes an experience for him of gradually penetrating a land in which he acquires an understanding of himself. The liberation that the mechanic dreams of—and here Tournier furnishes him with the very language of the surrealists—ends with the ecstatic union of love and destruction of the beloved object (*TO,* 102). Since Tournier systematically pushes surrealism in the direction of an interpretive delusion and drafts the plot in such a manner that it repeatedly affirms this delusional system of signification, National Socialism and its collapse become the end point of a process of self-development. The surrealist project of liberation is exposed as an unconfessed phantasm of destruction.

The juxtaposition of *The Ogre* with surrealist representations of desire casts the latter in an ironic light that simultaneously illuminates my resistance to the novel. The hopes that were tied to the May revolt of 1968 were also ones for the liberating power of desire. Institutions stood opposed to that power as hardened structures wholly alien to the subject. The revolt served to break open these structures and replace them with others more congenial to desire. An old (bourgeois) longing had almost acquired material force. If the fulfillment of this longing, however, is thinkable only as a delusion that fantastically projects its own desire onto reality so that reality becomes a mirror of that desire, then what is the status of the liberating power of desire? And if, in addition, longing for the other is inseparable from the will to destroy the other, if the wish for self-development is closely related to one for self-destruction, what remains then of the utopia of individual self-realization?

One could respond to such uncertainty by alleging that Tiffauges's delusional system is not the truth of surrealism. The latter is tied to a momentary breaking through of an entrenched consciousness of reality and certainly not to a closed system that transforms reality into a web of reciprocal references. And surrealism does not intend an obscuring of opposites, a lack of distinctions, but rather a synthesis of dream and reality in which difference is preserved.

Tournier, however, offers a response to such criticism in that his theory of inversion provides the protagonist with the possibility to maintain difference and, at the same time, to grasp its deeper unity, to recognize himself as both a friend of children and an ogre, a child-devouring monster. This is apart from the fact that he allows Tiffauges to comprehend his life, in good Hegelian fashion, as a sequence of stages in which what ensues sublates that which comes before: "Tiffauges avait toujours pensé que la valeur fatidique de chacune des étapes de son cheminement ne serait pleinement attestée que si, tout en étant dépassée et transcendée, elle se trouvait en même temps conservée dans l'étape suivante" (*RA*, 408); "Tiffauges had always thought the fateful significance of each step was fully attested to only if it was not merely surpassed and transcended, but also preserved in the subsequent stage" (*TO*, 262).

Tournier proceeds with *The Ogre* as he had in his first novel, *Friday*, in which he takes up the story of Robinson Crusoe in order to turn it into its opposite (Robinson learns about the joys of precivilized existence from Friday). Appropriating the surrealist project of destabilization, he turns that program against the utopia of a liberated existence insofar as he allows such an existence to be completely subordinated to a delusional system.

The insight expected of the reader—the renunciation of the discrete character of illusions—is not independent of Tournier's means of representation. The irritation that such means arouse in the reader renders material and concrete the reader's resistance and stimulates a process of reflection whose aim might very possibly be self-enlightenment.

Does this rescue the novel's aesthetic character? Hardly. The closed nature of the novel remains a problem. It can be expressed as follows: Tournier succumbs to the trap of the very figure he created. Tiffauges's paranoid world of signs is, strictly speaking, meaningless, since there are no gaps into which meaning could settle. Everything is always already interpreted by the protagonist. By contrast, Moosbrugger, Musil's mad murderer of prostitutes, fascinates us because the gazes of other figures are directed toward him. Tournier avoids such a rupture. The novel becomes a fixed and torpid portrait; all movement is feint, since it demonstrates only the ambivalent nature of the protagonist—something that was spoken about in the opening lines of his journal at the novel's beginning. Even National Socialist Germany is but one element in the process of Abel Tiffauges's self-discovery.

The torpidity of this delusional system of meaning renders *The Ogre* dependent on a receptive consciousness that sets the text in movement anew and allows it to become an instrument of recognition—a recognition, to be sure, that would not occur without the book but is, at the same time, not to be read from the book. In and of itself, *The Ogre* does not set anything in motion, and in that regard, it sets itself apart from the great texts of the modern literary age; only in confrontation with other texts does it unfold the power of its objection. We tested that power with surrealism, but it can also be shown with the classic bildungsroman and Proust's *Recherche*. The identity that the protagonist of the bildungsroman acquires through confrontation with the world appears in the pages of *The Ogre* as the incomplete impression left by a stabilized delusion. And Proust's trust in analogy as a process that subjects reality to the laws of the imagination can be read as suggestively anticipating the universal world of signs in which Tiffauges lives. Finally, we have already come up against the underlying similarities that link Tournierian protagonists with the Hegelian system. The effectiveness of Tournier's novel is based upon a game of inversion to which he summons the reader.

Collective Madness

We live in the time after National Socialism. Only gradually do we begin to sense what that means. Perhaps this irritating fascination with the phenomenon can be interpreted as a marker that we have begun to recognize in it—regardless of attempts to explain it in economic, political, and sociopolitical terms—something other than an event that falls outside the history of modern bourgeois society, namely, the realization of a collective madness and thus something like the backside of our reason.

The existence of a collective madness within modernity is, for the moment, merely an intuition suggested by Tournier's novel. If it can be corroborated, then the claim of truth bound to a notion of consensus would prove to be suspect. In order to discuss the matter, it is necessary first to develop a concept of madness.

When the French psychoanalyst Jacques Lacan returned to the issue of paranoia, which had been the subject of his doctoral dissertation in the 1930s, he developed his concept of madness in connection with Hegel's exposition about the Law of the Heart.[6]

Lacan asserts, in contradistinction to the common view that one who is mad deceives himself about himself, that any person who presumes to be one with his social role is no less mad, that "if a person who regards himself as a king is crazy, then a king who considers himself a king is no less mad." The essence of madness is not to be found in self-deception but rather in the immediacy of identification. In the *Phenomenology of Spirit,* Hegel had observed nothing other than that when he defined madness as the "law of the heart," the figure of self-consciousness "that assumes to have within itself the immediate universal or the law" (*PG,* 280).

Hegel (and also Lacan) does not persist in situating madness in the immediacy of a consciousness that knows itself to be self-identical, but rather, he traces its movement as it seeks to realize itself as the law of the heart. The necessity for doing so is imposed upon it, since the law of the heart is not the legitimate order of the world, and reality confronts consciousness as alien, as a "violent ordering of the world that contradicts the law of the heart" (*PG,* 275). Insofar as the law of the heart realizes itself, it ceases, nonetheless, to be the law of the heart. For consciousness does not introduce its law into reality, but rather, as Hegel says, it is imbricated in the real order. Since consciousness maintains itself in this manner, it is unable to recognize that the law of the heart may legitimately leave its mark on the world.

Consciousness, which acknowledges the law only in the law of its heart or "the universal only in the form of being for itself" (*PG,* 277), does not recognize itself in the existing order, which, nevertheless, is "its own essential being and work" (*PG,* 279). Consciousness thus comes into conflict with itself, since it does not recognize the existing order as its essence but rather seeks its essence only within itself. For Hegel, the result is madness. Insofar as that consciousness, which only follows the law of its heart, negates reality and the essence of the existing order, it simultaneously knows that what it negates is real and essential. Whereas consciousness belongs to two sets of essences, the law of the heart and the existing order, and whereas it fixes or defines the latter, it is "intrinsically contradictory and dirempted at its innermost" (*PG,* 279).

Hegel can define "the immediate singularity of consciousness that intends to be universal" as madness, since for him normal consciousness ultimately experiences the "way of the world to be not as evil as it appeared" (*PG,* 290). This experience is no longer ours; more likely, the opposite proves to be true: The way of the world is as evil as it appeared. In the final stages of this inversion, it follows that what Hegel defined as madness—individual consciousness that without mediation posits itself as the universal—is the historical figure of truth. Adorno's rescue of the subject proceeds along this line of argumentation. But is this final inversion not oversimplified if, implicitly at least, the existing order is characterized as mad? Does the same lack of insight into its own mediations—something that characterized the law of the heart for Hegel—not come with that inversion? If our experience is no longer the Hegelian one that "the way of the world is not as evil as it appeared," if consciousness mediated by the existing order is no longer certain of the reasonableness of the way of the world (without understanding this already as a necessary catastrophe), then it becomes a matter of developing criteria that would allow the reasonableness or unreason of a given order to be determined, that is, to consider collective madness as a deviation (not a condition of the world). It remains to be asked whether

Hegel's determinations of individual consciousness might be of help in this matter.

For Hegel, madness is strictly an individual phenomenon; it coincides with an individuality that is unable to see through its own mediation of the societal whole, that no longer recognizes in its own ideal the inverted mirror of what is actually the case. Hegel thereby stresses that in madness it is not consciousness as such but rather an object for consciousness that is deranged. If the real and essential is unreal and inessential for delusional consciousness, then it possesses consciousness of a reality and an essence that it nonetheless considers unreal. Insofar as consciousness establishes something simultaneously as real and unreal, essential and nonessential, it is dirempted.

A thoroughly comparable diremption can be observed in National Socialism's theories of race. This by no means consists merely in a false appraisal in which something that is not real (race as a characteristic complex that determines the collective) is considered real, but rather that this appraisal is known *simultaneously* to be real and unreal. Those who live under the delusion of race insist that belonging to the race defines the essence of the individual and know at the same time that race is a construction that can be arbitrarily imposed. "I determine who is a Jew." This sentence by Göring is not a somewhat cynical unmasking of himself; instead, it is the one side of a delusion, whose other side is the belief in the superiority of the German race. Toward the end of World War II, when whatever German youth capable of defending the country had been decimated, young Czech, French, and Polish men, who satisfied Himmler's notions of race, were brought to Germany; after training in the Napolas, it was expected that they would become German nationals. The aim of this initiative was to strengthen the German race. The objective, race, becomes in that moment an act of construction.[7]

The other determining characteristic that Hegel offers of the individual's madness—that the individual knows himself to be one and the same with the universal—exists as well in collective madness. To be sure, there is a decided difference. The law of the heart, once realized, ceases to be the law of the heart. It become a universal power, "for which this particular heart is a matter of indifference, so that the individual by setting up his own ordinance no longer finds it to be his own" (*PS*, 223). Such consciousness is deranged, insofar as it is unable to recognize itself in the real order, the production of which it has actively played a part.

If, however, individual consciousness recognizes the law of the heart in the world it has aided in forming, does it then acquire the objectivity that, according to Hegel, characterizes normal consciousness? Such consciousness has been enveloped by the world and knows that this is the only possible manner in which it can realize itself. It recognizes the world from which it knows it is separated as its world, which it legitimately regards as the essential. But is that not the same structure of consciousness of the normal bourgeois individual and that of the National Socialist who knows he is part of the "movement"? Is there a collective madness at all?

There is indeed a collective madness, and its derangement lies in the immediacy with which the individual existing in such a state knows himself to be one not only with the ideal but also with the consciousness of all other individuals of the collective. The delusion exists in the fact that alienation is sublated for the individuals within the collective. They live in the full enjoyment of knowing that they themselves are the ideal, that they are realizing this ideal, and that this knowledge is confirmed and mirrored thousandfold by all of those who exist in the same state of immediacy.

What is it about, this ecstatic oneness of experience that prevents the individuals from lapsing into conflict with each other for the sake of particular recognition? That is quite simply the mechanism of *erecting boundaries*. Every collective is defined by cutting itself off from others; the collective that exists in madness needs the other as the enemy. Enemies are those who deny the ideal that is supposed to be realized. Further, there is the charismatic figure of the leader who embodies the oneness of the collective. Finally—and for me this is decisive—there is a universe of signs independent of reality. In reality, the interests of individuals conflict with those of others even within the collective and do not allow the experience of immediate singularity to develop into something universal. When the actions of individuals occur wholly within the realm of signs, they can, however, experience jointly the realization of their ideal. Only in the world of signs can such a harmony of hearts emerge, something that in the modern age has become particularly compelling. This is because the dual antagonism of the individual with the other and of the individual with the world appears to be sublated, whereby this appearance is nothing other than a truth experienced by the individual wholly enclosed within the collective.

What gives us the right to denounce the truth experienced by the subject as mere appearance? The individual existing in collective madness has a contradictory image of himself. On the one hand, he is outside of himself, secure in his ecstatic harmony with the "führer" and those of a like mind. On the other hand, he also recognizes himself as an isolated individual (who is never able to forget, even as he marches at the party convention under its banner, that he is a small vegetable supplier from Ulm). On the one hand, he knows that he is at one with the ideal; on the other, that he is once again eternally separated from it. This split consciousness that experiences unity with the others as reality but also recognizes it as something not real, that knows that this shared world of signs is both essential and inessential, is madness. Within such an individual, the world of signs becomes a place of existence residing alongside existence.

If the individual in the modern age experiences the existing order as strange and the other as enemy, and if, at the same time, he knows that the order is a precondition of his being and that the other is one from whom he requires recognition, then modern consciousness is contradictory per se. The diremption, which, in line with Hegel, we denounced as constitutive of madness, is then rediscovered in the structure of modern consciousness. For Hegel, derangement consisted in an insistence on the law of the heart, as consciousness established the existing order simultaneously as invalid and essential. That, however, is the structure of modern consciousness, as it experiences the existing order as strange and yet knows that order to be a condition of its existence.

The conflict between modern consciousness and a delusional one would then seem to be resolved. It is reduced to a single distinction: the conflict between mediation and immediacy. While modern consciousness recognizes that it is mediated and traces each experience of immediacy back to its own mediation, the delusional one exists completely within the realm of immediacy. In those instances in which modern consciousness grasps the existing order from differentiated points of view, the delusional consciousness experiences contradictions as identical, since it never exists outside a state of immediacy. The vegetable supplier marching at the party convention negates the particularity of all contradictions and confirms in the same moment their identity with the ideal.

As distinct objects, modern consciousness and madness are also closely related. Their proximity is founded upon the dual alienation of the modern individual from the existing order and from the other. The desire for a sublation of alienation derives from this, and this desire is the driving force both of thinking and of social activism. *If there is such a thing as the heroism of modern consciousness, then it is to be found in the endurance of alienation;*

the delusional consciousness leaps beyond the horizon of desire and recognizes its accord with the goal of that desire. As such, desire burns in the fire of an experience of immediate unity with the ideal and with the other. Delusion is thus a figure of the consciousness of the modern.

If the thought process we have carried out in response to Tournier's *The Ogre* is sound, if it is true that collective delusion is a figure of modern consciousness because longing for sublation of a dual alienation is its driving force and because the delusion is nothing other than the lived realization of this longing, then it becomes discernible that fascism, insofar as it can be defined as a collective delusion, does not represent a regression to the archaic or premodern but rather a phenomenon of the modern. Only when we see that in fascistic delusion lies the inverted consciousness of the modern, only when we recognize (in the fascist collective) our desire for sublation of alienation, can we hope to lend our need for immediacy something other than political form.

Hegel, the theorist of the modern, who assumed a posture toward the negative—namely, desire, battle, madness, and death—which most philosophers of the Enlightenment sought to avoid; Breton, who through the autonomy of art sought to discover the potential to overcome the alienation of bourgeois everyday existence; and Tournier, who pens the inversions of philosophical novels: the three have at first glance nothing in common. And yet via the principle of inversion and the theme of delusion, their paths intersect. Certainly, inversion, which for Hegel is the principle of dialectical movement and thus of life itself, is viewed by the surrealists as an instrument for revolutionizing living conditions and by Tournier as a means to dislodge the foundations of Western self-consciousness. While for Hegel madness leads to a dirempting of individual consciousness and the site of reason always remains opposed to the collective or the "I that is a we," the surrealists invert this relationship. Precisely because they saw the First World War as exposing the irrationality of society, they had confidence in the creative power of individual madness and stood up against the ostracism of such individuals. Tournier inverts yet again the surrealist inversion and steers us back inside the boundaries of bourgeois normalcy, which, insofar as normalcy is based upon a world of independent signs, is indistinguishable from the delusional world of its hero.

Tournier, Breton, Hegel—what allows these authors to be brought into a constellation in which ultimately surrealism, fascism, and a philosophical notion of the modern mirror one another in inverted fashion? Does Tournier's text actually cite these other texts, or is it more likely the case that the formative history of the one writing rediscovers itself in Tournier's text? Or is it perhaps the "Now" of our historical predicament that calls for a reading of the Tournierian book—a predicament in which doubt about the grand utopia of desire becomes just as apparent as the insight into the minuscule difference that separates the modern consciousness of alienation from the delusion of its possible sublation?

3. The Thinking of the Master

George Bataille between Hegel and Surrealism

A Smile

In the beginning was a smile, an irritating smile, in no way comparable to the masculine activity of the smiling in one's beard with which the scientists in Musil's *A Man without Qualities* follow the talk in Diotima's salon. Theirs is the expression of deference and incompetence. In vain, I seek a similarly apropos phrase to define the smile in question here that always appears on the lips of the advocates of poststructuralism when one intends to propose an argument. So arrives the thought that to understand poststructuralism means nothing other than to understand this smile.

Hegel's Refutation

"to commence with the owl of Minerva" (Bataille's note)

If Hegel's owl of Minerva is truly the emblem of philosophy, then philosophical thought always arrives too late. Bataille, however, intends to think life. In 1937, the forty-year-old Bataille drafted a letter to Alexander Kojève, whose lecture on Hegel's *Phenomenology of Spirit* from 1933 to 1939 not only had led to a new assessment of Hegel in France but also had conferred upon the lecturer an extraordinary intellectual authority. Many significant intellectuals of the subsequent generation counted themselves among Kojève's listeners: the writer Raymond Queneau, the phenomenologist and long-time comrade of Sartre Merleau-Ponty, the sociologist Raymond Aron, the psychoanalyst Lacan, and even Bataille. The letter, which he never completed but nonetheless forwarded to the addressee, was nothing less than a claim to refute Hegel. "I imagine that my life—its abortion, or even better, the open wound that is my life—alone constitutes the refutation of Hegel's closed system" (5:396).[1]

The assertions that Bataille makes about his life ("abortion," "open wound") can be found in Artaud, whose letter exchange with Jacques Rivière published in 1925 in the *Nouvelle Revue Française* Bataille could have known. When Artaud remarks, "I suffer," when he speaks of the poison of existence (*le poison de l'être*), his remarks have a determinable referent, his mental illness. But what is Bataille speaking about? While for Artaud ineffable suffering seeks a linguistic expression that is denied him, it seems as if Bataille exploits the formula of pathos for a suffering creature only to refute Hegel's system. Or is the discourse more likely an attempt to assert the claim of autonomous thought even against the philosopher par excellence?

Apparently, Kojève had led listeners to believe that history had ended with Napoleon and philosophy with Hegel; in other words, historical quarrel had come to an end. Bataille takes things up at this point. If a person is essentially one who acts, that is, is negativity, then what becomes of that person when there is no longer any possibility for world-historical action? Insofar as he defines himself as useless negativity (*negativité sans emploi*), Bataille transforms the philosophical problem into one about the legitimacy of his own existence. Kojève might have responded to him that from a historical perspective, the individual is worthy of being neglected. What Bataille would explain at length is that he himself is just that (mediocre, of an insignificance without appeal).

Two movements characterize Bataille's texts as well as others. The author pushes devaluation of the self to thoughts of suicide ("What I have to say about it engages one to think that a misfortune occurs and that is all"; 5:370), but apparently that provides him with a power to assert his autonomy. The text slides from the level of the theoretical to that of the personal, only to interpret anew the latter theoretically. When Bataille writes, "I have no other self-justification than that of a shrieking animal whose foot has been caught in a trap" (5:370), he is speaking about himself and at the same time making an anthropological statement: The human, in accordance with its being, is never satisfied in its desires. "Sovereign desire, consuming and nourishing anguish, engages being, my being, to search beyond itself: nothingness" (6:317) reads a later text. In Hegel's *Phenome-*

nology of Spirit, desire is a figure of self-consciousness, but certainly an undeveloped one. Desire seeks to destroy the object so as to assert its own self-certainty but experiences instead the independence of the object and its very dependence on the object, which always arises anew for desire. One cannot imagine that satisfaction is impossible, Bataille states (6:293). Hegel imagines that himself but restricts the thought in such a manner that it is valid only for a self-consciousness that is mired in the stages of desire. Should then the attempt to refute Hegel ultimately come down to preserving and hypostatizing ontologically a stage in the experience of self-consciousness?

"Sovereign desire, which both devours and nourishes anguish, drives being, my being, to seek something beyond it: nothingness." "Being, my being," the formulation demonstrates once again that when Bataille uses the personal or possessive pronoun, he is addressing the individual as the universal, that is, an ontological statement based upon a personal experience. Insofar as he makes the authenticity of his experience the basis of his thinking, he introduces simultaneously an illegitimate element into the philosophical debate.

Listeners to Bataille's lecture on sin, from which this citation is taken, reacted variously to this demand. While some were immediately convinced by the sincerity that they perceived in Bataille's voice ("What strikes me in the discussion is Bataille's turn of voice, it seems to me absolutely authentic"; 6:331), others, such as the philosophers Hyppolite and Sartre, tended rather to regard this "inner sincerity" as a kind of cement for a philosophical reasoning that was lacking. Sartre, in particular, pushed Bataille into a corner, whereupon the latter frankly admitted the weakness of his position. If the attempt to express inner experience destroys that experience, then the position of those who undertake such an attempt is an impossible one. "I am speaking of an untenable position" (6:345).[2] Sartre admits the validity of that position but persists in speaking about experience as if language were a transparent medium (something that Bataille had just denied). Bataille does not address the inherent contradiction of Sartre's comment; rather, he represents his own position somewhat defensively. Instead of emphasizing his own unorthodox position, he submits himself to his adversaries' demands for consistency and allows himself to be examined by them so as in the final analysis to deem himself a Hegelian: "I've made no mystery of the fact that I am more than anything else Hegelian and without being so through and through" (6:348). Should the observation be attributed to a momentary requirement of the argument? Can it not also be read as evidence that

Bataille himself was aware that any serious anti-Hegelianism must first of all be Hegelianism?[3]

Two forms of speaking, which are at the same time forms of thinking, collide: philosophical argumentation that makes distinctions among concepts, expects deductions, and demands conclusions, and a thinking that refuses to perform the separation between individual experience and universal statement. While only those who have submitted to the discipline of philosophical argumentation can participate in it, that is, have abandoned the illusion that immediate experience can be of philosophical relevance, the confidence lives on in Bataille that there must be a thinking that would be the thinking of life.

The Surrealistic Impulse

Bataille is said to have based his refusal in the 1920s to participate in the organized discussion of the surrealists on the anacoluthon, "too many shitty idealists."[4] And after renegade surrealists had formed a group around Bataille, Breton felt compelled in the second Manifesto to call Bataille "the one sitting in the library." (Exercising a sedentary activity must have been absolutely despicable to the surrealists.) Those same polemics served more likely to mask similarities in their approach, something, so far as I can tell, Bataille never denied. In an early review of a surrealist volume of poetry, Bataille defined the surrealist project as a will to overstep boundaries in both thought and deed, which, at the same time, outlines his own project.[5] A note from the time of World War II reads, "I identify experience and consciousness" (5:473). The surrealist demand could not be formulated any more precisely: a unity of experience and knowledge. Like the surrealists, Bataille does not intend to produce works but rather to plumb the possibilities of experience: "The act of writing viewed as a means of writing," he notes in *Principes de rhetorique* (5:459). The impulse to which Bataille's thinking is indebted, insofar as it will be something more than philosophy, is a surrealist one. A passage from his Nietzsche book expresses just that: "The movement that is expressed is perhaps no longer in objects. It is, if one wishes, in my books" (6:205).

A difference deserves to be maintained: While Breton stakes everything on poesy becoming practical in the hope that potentials siphoned off into poetry can be used to change the everyday as expressed by Rimbaud's "changer la vie," Bataille rejects poesy because it oversteps boundaries only symbolically instead of actually living that overstepping; "poesy approaches sovereignty but runs aground on that which it evokes instead of life" (5:476). The conflicting regard each apparently has for poesy derives nonetheless from the same impulse that Foucault called transgression.[6]

In the mid-1930s, following the failure of the *Contre-attaque* movement, which was initiated jointly by Bataille and Breton, signs of a return to a traditional notion of poetry could be discerned among the surrealists. Bataille, by contrast, ventured into a radicalized phase with the founding of the secret society Acéphale and the Collège de Sociologie. The surrealists and especially Aragon toyed with a modern mythology.[7] Bataille and his friends took such thought in earnest. They wanted to form a new religion, or at least create the conditions for one. True to the surrealist principle of combining experience and knowledge with practical ends, the Collège de Sociologie sought to investigate social forms in which the sacred appeared in modern society and to free simultaneously the energies contained therein.[8]

The late Bataille judged the goal of founding a religion quite harshly: "an untenable preoccupation," "a monstrous error" (6:369, 373). As such, he restricted himself to highlighting the contradiction between an ecstatic conception of religion and the project's model of action: "the impossibility of a project from the moment in which everything is in play" (6:373). In other words, Bataille criticizes the efforts of the Collège de Sociologie because it joins the rational, goal-oriented categories of the project with the sphere of the sacred. But does the problem of such an undertaking not lie elsewhere, namely, in the attempt to retrieve premodern categories of the sacred for a society that has cast off its metaphysical ties?

It is precisely this concept of the modern that is questioned by Bataille. Already in the early essay *La Notion de dépense,* he links Marcel Mauss's category of the offering, which is derived from so-called primitive societies, to the modern and seeks evidence thereby to demonstrate that the modern has a false image of itself.[9] The ultimate aim of human endeavor in modern societies is not self-preservation but rather expenditure (*dépense*). The young man from an affluent house who has squandered his father's fortune may have "an interest in remarkable losses," but he cannot justify that interest according to a logic of useful endeavor. Bataille comes to his aid: For one, there is an excess of energies and goods in society that must be spent; for another, there can be no final aim of so-called useful endeavors. The final aim, therefore, can only be one that lies beyond the calculation of usefulness—in expenditure and catastrophe. To be sure, in modern society there are types of activities that can only be measured by the concept of unproductive expenditure. That also holds for artistic production (*dépense symbolique*) as well as for revolution (bleeding and utterly limitless social expenditure).[10]

Bataille, however, goes one step further. He explores the concept of *unproductive expenditure* not only for purposes of description but also to critique modern society insofar as this society does not declare itself for the principle of expenditure. Only from this perspective is the thought comprehensible that the archaic practice of sacrifice can solve the problem of the modern individual.

To the extent that he posits his own experience as that of the (modern) person, Bataille knows that this person is hopelessly alone and suffers from this solitude. He has seen through the aims of activity offered to him by society (means, power, recognition) and deemed them void. The realm of historical action is barred him (if he goes along with Kojève's thesis about the end of history, and Bataille does so). In this predicament, only two roads are open to him: That of an individual overstepping boundaries and that of a collective project for a new society. Bataille pursues the first with his erotic texts as he does theoretically with *L'Expérience intérieure;* the second he pursues with the project of founding a religion.

Whereas expenditure follows the logic of a desire for self-destruction, without ever achieving it, sacrifice, or more precisely human sacrifice, founds a society among its participants. Through the death of the one sacrificed, they experience their own deaths.

> *Le sacrifice est la communication de l'angoisse [. . .]. A fin qu'en moi cette existence donnée aux hommes cesse d'être stérilement fermée et* communique, *il était nécessaire qu'un autre meure devant moi. Et non seulement devant moi mais devant d'autres en chaque chose semblables à moi et, comme moi, adhérents par l'angoisse à l'anéantissement qui a lieu.* (5:442n)

> Sacrifice is communication of anguish [. . .]. So that in me this existence given to humankind ceases to be infertilely closed and *communicates,* it was necessary that another die in front of me. And not simply in front of me but in front of others who were like me in every way and who like me were handed over to the annihilation that was taking place.

Bataille does not refer to the Christian idea of symbolic sacrifice but rather to pre-Christian rituals of sacrifice. The symbolic sacrifice of Christianity appears to Bataille to lack the experience of anguish that founds community and to burden with guilt those who are excluded from that good deed (cf. 6:329).

Just as Bataille never finished the letter to Kojève and only later published it in part, so did he not publish that section about sacrifice. Beyond that, he added a note to the text that explicitly rejected a literal understanding: "It is about a complicity with death and only with that which is revealed in spiritual anguish, not in acts to be accomplished" (5:445).

On the other hand, the text has the tenor of a writ of initiation. And it was reported by the Acéphale that its arcanum was a yet-to-be-realized human sacrifice. The interpreter is confronted with a structure that can be characterized as fundamentally ambiguous. Certainly, Bataille is serious about what he writes. But this seriousness is one that is revoked at each moment. Sartre would interpret that as *bad faith.* Is this interpretation compelling, or does it force Bataille's thinking to be considered according to a schema that it immediately argues against? Avoiding the logic of either/or, one can perhaps say the following: Bataille's thinking has something somnambulistic about it; in a word, it crashes. That suspicion may well have prompted him to develop the double gesture of a fractured radicalism.

"Ces Forces Noires"

In June 1940, after a walk along the Place de la Concorde, Bataille noted, "It is the place of the Terror. I concede all rights to the people. Let the people immolate every life according to the necessity, glorious or not, that the people carry within" (5:524).

In the years before the Second World War, the work of the Collège de Sociologie declined. In France, the people's front collapsed; in Germany, Hitler was at the pinnacle of his success. The analyses of Bataille and Caillois revolve around the thought of the necessity of a *spiritual power.* In the beginning of 1939, Bataille held a lecture in the Collège, "Hitler and the Teutonic Order." The lecture is not preserved, but an outline of his thoughts, which he presented to Caillois in a letter, allows one to recognize that he grants Hitler's attachment to the *ordre teutonique* a mythical character ("the affiliation to the teutonic order is probably 'mythic' "), but at the same time, he seeks an answer to the elite schools of National Socialism, which he grasps as part of a military order.[11] France had nothing with which to oppose the National Socialist myth, but it could protect itself against the militarily organized structure of submission that had installed itself in Germany.

The Collège envisioned constituting itself as an *ordre,* as the church or a moral congregation through which it could then claim spiritual authority. The question whether the National Socialists had realized this project in its own fashion had yet to be decided. If the mythical character of the *ordre teutonique* could not be denied, then it had realized a *pouvoir spirituelle,* but one that Bataille and his friends certainly could not accept for themselves. The thought of a mythically legitimated power, once realized, confronted them as something hostile. The community of the strong, which they had hoped to form, was already in place, but as one that was directed against them.

Boris Souvarine, at whose Marxist-oriented periodical *La Critique sociale* Bataille had worked, asserted in a later text that Bataille had been fascinated with Hitler in the 1930s but had prudently refrained from making his position public.[12] The hatred for Bataille that issues from the text of the older Souvarine casts doubt on his evidence. Nonetheless, the notion of fascination might have touched upon something. In order to avoid any misunderstanding, it is not a question of whether Bataille had acquainted himself with what at the time was known as *hitlérisme:* that is certainly not the case. "[I]n agreement with the hate of Hitlerism," he wrote in 1939 to Caillois (*LRC,* 121). But it would be too simple to suggest that by reference to this passage the matter has been settled.[13] More likely, it is a matter of pursuing an affinity of Bataille's mode of thinking with something that he himself did not recognize in National Socialism, namely, its fascist philosophy.[14] Bataille had always understood that there was something risky about his thought. Whoever decides to become involved with his thinking ought to know the risks.

In October 1939 Jean Paulhan, the editor of the *Nouvelle Revue Française,* who also followed carefully the work of the Collège de Sociologie, wrote to Roger Caillois:

> *Je vois bien sur quels points (au demeurant Bataille l'a assez marqué) l'hitlérisme peut s'accorder avec les thèses du C[ollège de] S[ociologie]. Quand ce ne serait que par ce pouvoir accordé à ceux qui s'en sentent dignes. Je vois moins clairement ce qui vous donne le droit de le traiter d'abcès à vider.* (as cited, *LRC,* 122n)

> I see quite well what points (Bataille has underscored them quite clearly) of Hitlerism are compatible with the thesis of the C[ollège de] S[ociologie]. Less clear to me is who gives you the right to handle it as an ulcer that should be removed.

Caillois's answer, which he also understood to be Bataille's, turns out to be a particularly weak one. What prevents him from turning to Hitlerism is its racism.

> *L'hitlérisme est un idéal qui ne premet pas qu'on y adhère. It faut la grâce, et celle-ci n'est pas la récompense de la vertu, mai une donnée de la naissance.* (as cited, *LRC*, 124)
>
> Hitlerism is an ideal that does not permit adherents. It requires grace, and this is not recompense for virtue but something given at birth.

In other words, one cannot choose National Socialism, one is born into it. A French person cannot stand for an ideal that is based upon the claims of superiority of the German race. Caillois's second argument juxtaposes ethical values such as choice, elective affinity, and merit with the facticity, compulsion, and immutability that serve as the principles of allegiance to National Socialism. Apparently, Caillois and Bataille consider the yet-to-be-created *ordre* one of moral self-selection and not a community of fate.

Insofar as we hold to this difference, we run the risk of passing over Bataille's radicalness—one that is perhaps most remarkably expressed in the short text, *La Menace de guerre* (*The Threat of War*), which he published unsigned in June 1939 in his journal *Acéphale*. While heads of Western democracy had acceded to Hitler in Munich in 1939 in order to preserve the peace, Bataille's text announced the following: Struggle is life; death, the completion of life; war, an event that transcends the significance of its causes. The "church" that could legitimately be created would realize itself in war. Its values are tragic, for the catastrophe cannot be meaningless.

> 1. Struggle is the same thing as life. The value of a man depends on his aggressive force.
> 2. A "vital" man views death as that which finishes life: he does not view it as a misfortune.
>
> [. . .]
>
> 6. The values of this church should be of the same order as the traditional evaluations that place tragedy at the summit: independently of political results, it is impossible to view a descent into hell of the human universe as deprived of meaning. (1:550)

The text maintains a distance from fascism, which slavishly subordinates all values to struggle and work: "Fascism servilely subordinates every value to work and struggle" (1:551). But it is precisely this distinction that renders the text bewilderingly ambiguous despite its aim toward univocity. If in one moment struggle appears as life's loftiest value, in the next it appears as something to be rejected along with work. No less bewildering is the combative pathos and readiness for catastrophe that issue from other texts by the Collège de Sociologie.[15]

In the face of fascism's threat, Bataille radically transforms his idea of expenditure into a theory of pure struggle that no longer pursues a political aim but rather puts into play the fate of humanity. For Bataille, the only way to take action against fascism is apparently to push what he considers fascism's combative self-assertion toward pure expenditure. In a purely literal sense, it is a matter of mimesis of the inured (*Verhärtete*), of which Adorno speaks in another context. One does Bataille an injustice if one suppresses the lack of freedom, the compulsion, that is a part of his resistance.

In 1968, Caillois recalled his return to Paris after the war:

> *Le guerre nous avait montré l'inanité de la tentative de Collège de Sociologie. Les forces noires que nous avions rêvé de déclencher s'étaient libérées toutes seules, leurs conséquences n'étaient pas celles que nous avions attendues.* (as cited, *LRC,* 131n)
>
> The war has shown us the inanity of the Collège de Sociologie. The dark forces that we had dreamed of unleashing liberated themselves, but the consequences were not those that we had anticipated.

The Thinking of the Master or the Limits of Critique

Sartre, whose *Being and Nothingness* appeared in the same year as *L'Expériénce intérieure,* devoted an extensive discussion to Bataille's book. Bataille is concerned with an experience that leaves rational, directed action (the project) behind for the sake of a limit experience in which anguish and desire mix to the point of indecipherability. Sartre responded, "But we *are* project."[16] Only in the act of constructing a project is the subject constructed. To the extent that anthropological assumptions are set in opposition to each other, there is no movement in the debate. That first occurs as Sartre opens himself up to Bataille's thought in order to unmask that thought as the result of a linguistic deception. He demonstrates how Bataille progresses from the simple assertion of nonknowing to its substantialization (the night of nonknowing) in order to transform that into a kind of knowledge that delimits Hegel's absolute knowledge:

> And here the slippage I know nothing. Good. That means that my knowledges stop [. . .] But if I substantiate my ignorance, if I transform it into the night of nonknowing, there it becomes positive. I can touch it. I dissolve myself there. Having attained nonknowing, absolute knowledge is no more than one knowledge amongst others.[17]

In his reply, Bataille specifically and extensively cited this passage from Sartre's discussion and emphasized what was most striking. Sartre underlines, according to Bataille, what is inane in the movement of Bataille's thought—from the perspective of the outside (6:199). But just this, it reads a bit later, is inadequate to the interior experience, whose movement can be grasped only by one who shares it (6:199). Bataille immediately incorporates Sartre's critique into his own thinking and transforms it into a moment of restlessness, of an instance that arouses dizziness. As such, he describes his own thinking experience: "I could only draw from a well made criticism, as the case may be, a new form of anguish, partaking of intoxication" (6:199).

When Sartre reproaches Bataille for deception, insincerity, and fraud (*truquage, supercherie,* and *mauvaise foi*), he is arguing within the framework of a morality of honesty. Man is a project; he must assume that condition; if he does not, he persists in a state of indeterminacy, of *bad faith,* that is, of a poorly masked self-deception. Sartre even reproaches Bataille for the following: The contradictions that he constructs in his texts between the external perspective of the scientist and the inner perspective of one who experiences, between the will to self-affirmation and the will to self-deprecation. Such contradictions are for Sartre the expression of a passionately engaged indecisiveness (*mauvaise foi passionnelle*). The argument is based upon the assumption that *mauvaise foi* and *sincérité* are postures distinguishable from one another. That, however, is what Bataille questions. If man is essentially a contradiction, if knowledge about the death of God allows the need for transcendence to persist, then *mauvaise foi* is *sincérité* for him. The demand for the authenticity of experience ("Entering into the unsuspected region, I saw that which no eyes had ever before beheld"; 5:11) coincides with the confession that it depends upon an intervention of the will (Bataille talks about *dramatization* in this context). The immediate coincidence of contradictions, however, enfeebles critique. For that reason, any attack against Bataille's irrationalism is impotent and merely reinforces with its juxtaposed values what Bataille's text proclaims. Instead of criticizing Bataille's thinking as weak and contradictory—"as soon as one seeks to grasp it, [Bataille's thought] melts like snow"[18]—it becomes a matter of situating it in the relational field of dialectical thinking in order to clarify it.

"For there is in the heart of man an uneasiness that is not in the power of any god or woman to allay" (5:143). Bataille, who with this remark approaches the notion of Lacanian desire, offers an anthropological assumption. Man is not a project, as Sartre maintains, but rather unrest, uneasiness. That is, he is, from a metaphysical point of view, a being that is lacking. What he lacks is the possibility to arrive at the purity of peaceful contentment with himself and life. If one grants this basic assumption, the question arises as to how one gets along with his being and what does one make of it. Three "solutions beckon": One can attempt to deaden unrest (Schopenhauer's denial of the will), one can attempt to transform it into an impetus for inner-worldly activity (what Pascal as diversion and Bataille as project criticized), and finally, one can attempt to live and experience that unrest—and this is the course Bataille's philosophy pursues. And it is—insofar as one shares his basic assumption—no less plausible than the other two solutions; it can, in fact, claim that it alone assumes a position toward one's metaphysical *condition*. Herein may lie one of the reasons for the fascination that issues from thinking such as Bataille's in an epoch in which the idea of the figurability of history has truly faded.

Uneasiness as a condition corresponds to the certainty of one's own death. Everyday existence, drab existence, stands in opposition to both. Life must be wrested from it, life in the emphatic, ecstatic sense of the word, "it seems that we need nothing more than the small loss of death for the flash of life to traverse and transfigure drab existence" (5:142). There is true life only in death, but in death there is no life. How is it that death comes to life?[19] It can only be simulated. Anguish and the rapture of ecstasy are simulations of death. By way of them, the self comes to itself in that the self exposes itself. Bataille's accounts of inner experience do not fully agree with each other, but they nonetheless find concordance in their method of proceeding (dramatization) and in their transference of anguish into the joyous experience of ecstasy. This is first achieved in that moment in which the ego—or, as Bataille states, the self—is prepared to give itself up.

Who is the bearer of this experience? Sartre offers a sober answer to this question: a certain Mr. Bataille, librarian at the Bibliothèque Nationale. But insofar as this Mr. Bataille writes a text, he renders himself unrecognizable. There is thus nothing else to do save to seek an answer to this question in the text itself. As a result, the bearer of ecstatic experience is a proud self (*ipse fier*), capable of exposing himself. This self-exposure presents itself as *sovereign act* and points to the figure of the master, in which motifs of Hegel's and Nietzsche's thought are peculiarly mixed.

Kojève spoke disparagingly of the master in Hegel's *Phenomenology.* He could only die in battle or become a zombie in pleasure. Meaningful, historical action was purely the domain of the slave. But when the slave came to a bad end (under Stalin or Hitler), it was reasonable to turn renewed attention to the master. Unlike the slave, the master pursues no aim. A certain unrest may prod him to secure his self and his possibilities, but action wholly directed to a work is abhorrent and slavish. His action can only be something grandiose that exceeds all limits: the leap into death. But the master intends to live. Therefore, he must simulate his own death, he must tear himself apart and from that return to himself. Endless movement, desperate pleasure, pleasurable desperation. The master has made himself unassailable. While the critic attempts to apprehend him in one figure, he has already assumed another. Through his discourse, the critic demonstrates that he has no share in the master's universe. The master smiles.

The Split Self

Perhaps the difficulty in approaching Bataille's thought stems from the fact that the self that appears in his writing appears oddly undefined. It is neither the universal self of the scientist nor the fictive one of narration nor the personal self of autobiography, which could vouch for the authenticity of what is reported. In *L'Expérience intérieure,* Bataille speaks of mystical experiences, but this speech denounces its own vocabulary as mere excuses (*faux fuyants*). To speak of the experience means to turn away from it:

> *Mes yeux se sont ouverts, c'est vrai, mais il aurait fallu ne pas le dire, demeurer figé comme un bête. J'ai voulu parler, et comme si les paroles portaient la pesanteur de mille sommeils, doucement, comme semblant ne pas voir, mes yeux se sont fermés.* (5:25)

> My eyes opened themselves, it is true, but it would have been necessary not to say it, to remain frozen like an animal. I wanted to speak, but as if words carried the weight of a thousand slumbers, softly, as though seeming not to see, my eyes closed themselves.

If language belongs to the world of means and ends, what Bataille calls *project,* and if mystical conditions, by contrast, to a "silent, hidden, intangible part" of the self, then the self that speaks of experience is not the same self of experience.

> *Le "je" incarne en moi la chiennerie docile, non dans la mesure òu il est* ipse, *absurde, incommunicable, mais une équivoque entre la particularité de cet ipse et l'universalité de la raison.* (5:134)
>
> The "I" embodies in me a canine docility, not in the measure *ipse,* absurd, incommunicable, but as an equivocation between the particularity of this ipse and the universality of reason.

The self is not only the "law of language" and thus subject to the world of ends and work, but its position is also ambiguous, since the particular and the universal are intermingled in it. Opposed to this servile self, Bataille posits the "wild self" that proposes universals not according to the law of reason but according to the law of unreason (*déraison*). The bearer of ecstatic experience is the "ipse," but it is silent. So the "I" (*je*) must speak for it and thus necessarily betray its material.

The self that speaks of its experience can be neither the "ipse" nor the "je"; for the universe of speech is closed to the former and that of experience to the latter. Therefore, we read a text that secures its own impossibility. Stated otherwise, the self that says of itself, "I would have spoken," is an impossible self.

Bataille then posits in *L'Expérience intérieure* a series of procedures to authenticate the text. The most important of these procedures is the ironic relativization of his own text ("The only parts of this book urgently written [. . .] are the second, the Torture, and the last. I wrote this book with the laudable intention to write a book"; 5:9) as well as a change of registers (more or less from theoretical reflection to the reporting of experience) and the emphasis on a rupture ("The opposition to the idea of a project is so necessary in me, that having written a detailed plan for this introduction, I can no longer hold myself to it"; 5:18). The movement that Bataille often ironically or self-critically turns to in his own writing produces authenticity by means of self-depreciation. The proclaimed carelessness toward the form of the text and, by contrast, the effort exerted on the form of individual textual passages gives the reader the impression that he is concerned with something "more" than literature.

Behind the double of the *sovereign I* and the *servile I,* another figure is recognizable in some of the more strongly autobiographical texts. And one would be tempted to designate that self as the real one, were the structure of its autobiographical writing not so naively worked out. In *Le Surréalisme au jour le jour,* a text written in 1951 but never intended for publication, Bataille describes his relationship to the surrealists and offers, at the same time, an instructive (self) portrait of the young George Bataille. On the one hand, the young Bataille envied the surrealists due to their recognition as writers, which in contrast to his life as a librarian seemed like a life more true (8:177); he always maintained the suspicion that the movement might be a shrill fraud (*bruyante supercherie*). His divided attitude toward the surrealists corresponded to his own divided self-assessment. The feeling of inferiority, particularly in relation to Breton but also to Michel Leiris, who since his entry into the surrealists was the one who for Bataille was in on a secret from which he was excluded, was overlaid with lingering feelings of superiority. "I could only give myself over to a secret and enticing violence, which animated me, which dedicated me, I believe, to some visionary fate, worthy of interest" (8:171). "Personally, I was nothing if not the place of an empty agitation" (8:171). "The hidden and irritable violence" and "the empty agitation" befall the self that, however, only knows itself as such a site. Bataille does not react as Schopenhauer had to this experience by renouncing the will, but, in step with Nietzsche, he affirms it. Thereby ensues the rejection of the rational self as a figure of subjugation and the constitution of a self based on an affirmation of violence.

It is not in the manifest Nietzschean legacy that the particularity of Bataille's gesture lies but rather in his maintenance of a double determination of the self. He knows himself to be nothing and to be "all reality." And he knows himself to be one and the other simultaneously. He is, as Breton disparagingly noted, "one sitting in the library" and, at the same time (as violence), the principle of all life. When Bataille defined himself as "useless negativity" (5:396) in a 1937 letter to Kojève, he thus presented himself again in Hegelian terms as a self doubly determined, which, in looking back on the 1920s, the text on surrealism had unfolded. As negativity, he coincides with that which moves everything; as one for whom no historical perspective remains available (*sans emploi*), he must accept his irrevocable meaninglessness.

The double determination of the self tears the subject asunder. It disintegrates into a small contemptible ego and a grandiose self. Nothing separates the former from the world of the many, which, as the grandiose, disdains the ego, since its life passes on in subjection to the imperative of the useful. The grandiose self, which imagines itself as the master, stands, however, at the border of madness. It knows only unbridled expenditure. The unity of the two and the knowledge of that impossibility is uniquely captured by Bataille in "laughter," the gesture that radically places his thought in question without stripping it of its deadly seriousness.

4. The Master and His Angel

Approaches to Maurice Blanchot

Literature and Anguish

There is no thinking without presuppositions, only the attempt to catch up with the presuppositions of one's own thinking. This has a name: philosophy. In this respect, the literary theoretical essays of Maurice Blanchot are philosophy. They revolve around the possibility of literature being an existential experience.

> *Un écrivain qui écrit: "Je suis seul" ou comme Rimbaud: "Je suis réellement d'outre-tombe" peut se juger assez comique. Il est comique de prendre conscience de sa solitude en s'adressant à un lecteur et par des moyens qui empêchent l'homme d'être seul. Le mot seul est aussi général que le mot pain. Dès qu'on le prononce, on se rend présent tout ce qu'il exclut.*[1]

> A writer who writes, "I am alone" or like Rimbaud, "I am actually from beyond the grave" can seem a little ludicrous. It is comical to be aware of one's solitude while addressing a reader, making use of means that keep one from being alone. The word "alone" is as general as the word "bread." As soon as one utters it, one makes present everything that it excludes. (*Eng.*, 1)

The writer is alone and must pronounce this solitude ("The writer is not free to be alone without expressing that he is"; *FP,* 10; *Eng.*, 2). But in doing so, he is embroiled in an insoluble aporia. Since the medium he must use to express his solitude is essentially universal, he destroys by writing the situation that he would like to present. Since each text presumes a reader, a solitude that is written is at the same time its opposite, the virtual presence, at the very least, of a multiplicity of readers.

In the text, the two arguments cross with each other: a theoretical one about language that Blanchot takes from Hegel and a literary theoretical argument in which he refers to Valéry's critique about the demands for the authenticity of literature. In the *Phenomenology of Spirit,* Hegel demonstrated that language does not allow the concrete "this" of sense-certainty to be said, "because the sensuous This that is meant *cannot be reached* by language, which belongs to consciousness; i.e. to that which is inherently universal."[2] Since language inverts what is intended by turning the concrete into a universal, it thereby possesses a "divine nature." For Hegel, the unutterable is the untrue, the irrational. Blanchot, by contrast, understands the universality of linguistic expression in the sense of an aporia. While the one writing wants to preserve the concrete experience in all of its particularity, language forces him to negate even that.

The solitude of the one writing is thrown into question through the act of writing in yet another fashion. While he writes, he addresses a reader; that is, he instantiates his solitude for another: "To write is to enter on the scene— [. . .] One does not escape it," is found in a note of Valéry.[3] The writer, whose only demand upon himself is to lend his feelings expression, betrays himself through the care with which he tends to his linguistic expression. His sincerity is that of the playactor. That the problem of literary authenticity was not thereby settled for Valéry is evident from the intensity of his occupation with the object.[4] Just as he had inverted Hegel's assessment of the universal of linguistic expression, so Blanchot performs a makeover of Valéry's argument. If for Valéry the writer was a playactor, Blanchot sees him in a comic situation. Not that he acts out something that is not the case, but rather, he finds himself inevitably in contradiction with himself. He is alone but must destroy this solitude in the moment he pronounces it. Whereas Valéry advised the writer to give up any claim of authenticity, Blanchot holds onto that claim but sees it bound to the possible realization of its own destruction. Writing—so his thought seems to suggest—is not divorced from a radical solitude, but it is no less removed from an inevitable destruction of that solitude in the very act of writing.[5]

What sort of thought process is presented here? Can it be understood as a dialectic process? The solitary one would then be confronted with the command to lend his solitude the form of writing. The text, which is the result of this confrontation, would negate this solitude but at the same time preserve it by elevating it to the status of the universal. In other words, it has to do with the movement that Hegel called sublation. Undoubtedly, one can consider the linguistic aporia in the sense of Hegelian sublation. Blanchot, however, does not do so. The universal of linguistic formulation is not a higher stage in comparison with the particularity of lived solitude, nor is the demand to write conceived of as something that temporally succeeds solitude; lacking is the procedural character of thought. The contradictions coincide. The solitude of the writer is simultaneously its own destruction in the act of writing. It can be formulated only as follows: Blanchot grounds the authenticity of the writer in its impossibility. Thought is not given to movement but is brought to a halt in the preserved aporia.

Blanchot thus discovered the gesture of thought that allowed him to establish the impossibility of writing as a condition of its possibility. The writer, a being of radical solitude, is separated from all means of expression; he is nothing save his complete despair. At the same time he is conscious of this despair and the one who has words at his disposal ("the rest is bound to the arrangement of words"; *FP,* 10; *Eng.,* 2). He is not first "this" and then "that," but rather "this" and "that" together without the possibility of one being severed from the other. "It is even in the manner of his expression that he coincides best with the inexpressible nothingness that he has become" (*FP,* 10; *Eng.,* 2). We should not allow ourselves to be led astray by the "it has become," which seems to signal a development of sorts. It is not a matter of a process, of a progression from one stage to the next on the path of dialectical negation, but rather of a coincidence of opposites. As he writes, the writer has the experience of one for whom means of expression are refused, as "nothingness without expression." The writer betrays his dream of pronouncing the experience of solitude without mediation to the means of its realization, language. This, however, leaves him in the lurch by turning his project into its opposite. Realization of the dream is its relinquishment.

"How is literature possible?" reads the title of one of Blanchot's first theoretical attempts. What one understands as literature is not an exceptional communication distinguished by definite, formal features but rather an existential practice (praxis) in which experience and life coincide; as such, the title can be translated as follows: Is an authentic literature possible? Blanchot's answer is at first glance baffling in its simplicity. It is possible if I incorporate into the author the other, to whom linguistic expression is necessarily directed. If romantic thought characterizes the writer of experience, and neoclassical thought, by contrast, the one possessing technical control of language, Blanchot thinks these two perspectives together. The writer is the one who combines the existential experience of anguish with a command of language. Were he to exist merely in the immediacy of existential anguish, these experiences would simply not be for him. He must produce within himself the eloquent observer in order to be able to experience anguish.

> *L'existence de l'écrivain apporte la preuve que, dans le même individu, à côté d l'homme angoissé subsiste un homme de sang-froid, à côté du fou un être raissonable et, uni étroitement à un muet qui a perdu tous les mots, un rhéteur maître du discours.* (*FP,* 12)

> The existence of the writer brings with it the proof that, in the same individual, alongside the anguished being subsists a being of cold blood; alongside the madman, a reasonable man; and close-coupled with a mute who has lost all words, a master of rhetoric. (*Eng.*, 4)

Upon closer inspection, the solution to the problem seems only to be an apparent one. For the coexistence of an experiencing and of a writing self within the writer is precisely what summoned Valéry's derision of the comedy of sincerity. To be sure, Blanchot speaks of a coexistence, but the text points to the fact that he thinks of these moments of mutual conflict as a unity. The writer does not first experience anguish in order to articulate it later (that would only be a variation of the romantic relationship to expression), but rather, he is the anguish that must be spoken and yet remains unutterable. Anguish demands thereafter to be uttered, since otherwise it would not exist, or stated otherwise, since anguish is movement, "heart-rending movement," that only comes to itself in that it destroys itself. But it is ineffable insofar as each linguistic form that it can assume transforms it into something else. It is thus no longer that unmistakable existential experience but rather a work, a being, that is for others.

Blanchot places two mutually exclusive demands upon the writer. He should, on the one hand, be absolutely by himself in the immediacy of experiencing existential anguish and, on the other, articulate this experience. The possibility of a realization of this aporetic project—the meaningless work ("a book in which the putting into play of all his signifying forces is reabsorbed into the insignificant"; *FP,* 16; *Eng.*, 8) or the work that excludes the hypothetical reader—is understood by Blanchot to be artifice. Its deficiency lies in the certainty with which it excludes something (meaning, the reader) and with which it thereby refers precisely to that which through negation it is still attached. From Blanchot's point of view, ambiguity is defective for its lack of determinacy, something that only the text that combines absolute equivocity with a demand for univocity can overcome (*FP,* 17).

There is also no escape from the paradoxical situation of the writer, in the Kierkegaardian sense of the word, that would not have the form of the paradox. Since every successful work transforms the experience of anxiety into something else—a cultural value, an object of solace for others (*FP,* 14)—the writer must conceive of his work as failed. But since the intended failure would once again be a success, he must practice an art in which success and failure coincide. "The art he uses is an art in which perfect success and complete failure must appear as one" (*FP,* 13; *Eng.,* 5). Blanchot rejects the most radical formulations of art for art's sake as self-deception, because what was intended to be useless is always transformed from behind into something culturally useful. By contrast, to accord with anguish means producing a work—or, better, a nonwork—that remains connected to the act of its emergence and that does not become transformed into an object of value. Such a work would be, as Blanchot remarks in adopting a central concept of Bataille, expenditure.

> *L'écrivain est appelé par son angoisse à un réel sacrifice de lui-même. Il faut qu'il dépense, qu'il consume les forces qui le font écrivain. Il faut aussi que cette dépense soit véritable [. . .] Il est nécessaire qu'il soit détruit dans un acte qui le mette réellement en jeu.* (*FP,* 13)

> The writer is summoned by his anguish to an actual sacrifice of himself. He must expend and consume the forces that make him a writer. And this expenditure must be real [. . .] He must be destroyed in an act that actually puts him in play. (*Eng.,* 5)

Insofar as the writer expends himself by writing—that is, he actually destroys the ability that makes him a writer by putting everything into his work—the work remains, paradoxically, bound to his activity. It does not assume the character of an object, but it preserves the character of the act. Blanchot did not reflect his entire life in vain upon the *automatic writing* of the surrealists, in which the one writing offers himself up both as a writer and as a person.

Until now, we have proceeded descriptively. It was our aim to find entry into the uniquely sealed work of the young Blanchot. Its center, so it seems, is less a thought, a thesis, than a form of thought: the paradox. Contradictions collapse without mediation. Blanchot's thinking in *De l'Angoisse à la littérature* is a thinking without mediation. That is joined with a radical solipsism whose spokesperson the text makes itself out to be. The self of the writer is alone with himself. The moments of the one experiencing and of the one observing, into which the self separates under the gaze of Blanchot, does not change anything. The other, of which the text speaks, is merely the other side of the solitary self. In this guise, its ultimate aim is not to allow its existential solitude to be contaminated by the effects of the present. The self holds onto this aim at all costs, even at the risk of self-destruction.

In the text, mediation is the name of the evil that multifariously threatens the solitary one—mediation through the universality of linguistic expression and the object character of the work. In opposition to that, Blanchot summons the power of the paradox. It is the power of insetting (*Ineinsetzen*) opposites that draws the self out of estrangement from the other. Its logic of coincidence is destructive. "Paradox is the passion of thought. But the highest potency of any passion is always to will its own decline, and so it is also the extreme passion of reason to seek inducement, although that inducement must in some fashion lead to decline."[6]

For Kierkegaard, the destructive power of paradoxical thought creates a space for facts. It is different for Blanchot. Paradox is not a transitional stage but rather an endlessly extended moment of radical despair. Evidence of such is offered to the self in the form of revealing truth in which everything, not only the world and others but also the self, disappears as a particular something. The text maintains that position by turning anguish into an allegorical subject to whose demands the self subjects itself. The self that would pronounce its existential experience of anguish has made itself into an instrument of anguish, one that it is no longer able to pronounce even though that anguish is properly its own. The self has literally nothing to say. And that, however, makes it loquacious.

What allows the early solipsism of Blanchot to be understood? Kierkegaard is named in the text, and traces of Mallarmé's *Igitur* and Rimbaud's *Lettres du voyant* are recognizable. But such allusions to literary texts do not explain anything; they are rather in need of an explanation. Let us venture a hypothesis: When Blanchot published *De l'Angoisse à la littérature,* German troops had occupied France for years. Blanchot's engagement with the French Right was an issue of the 1930s. With the occupation of France, such a position becomes untenable. The will toward national renewal can be realized only by abandoning the goal in the very act of its realization. For the French Right, giving oneself up is the only form of self-realization.

Blanchot is not a collaborator, but he thinks its logic through to the end. No one else, no history, and no dialectic remains save for the subject of anguish that comes to itself only by giving itself up. Instead of directing the destructive power of solipsism outward by virtue of its own superiority, the self turns that force inward: to the rigorous work of the annihilation of the self, a self that once (so one will presume) thought to dictate the law of the heart to others and that maintains itself now only in the repeated gesture of self-annihilation.

Consciousness without a Subject

"All writers of bourgeois origin have known the temptation of irresponsibility: for a century that has been the tradition of the literary career."[7] With this sentence Sartre begins his 1945 preface to *Les temps moderne* and thereby subjects literature to a moral political imperative. Against the temptation of irresponsibility, he posits an obligation of engagement. "To write is to engage oneself; but to write is also to disengage oneself, to commit oneself irresponsibly," Blanchot replied in "Kafka et la littérature."[8] Rather than reject Sartre's thesis, Blanchot appears to affirm it ("to write is to engage oneself"), but only so as to interpret that thesis in such a manner as to reject it. How does one think about an engagement that is also a disengagement? An answer requires that one first clarify what literary engagement means for Blanchot.

For the modern writer, literature is literature, and writing is the ability to put well-ordered sentences to paper ("mettre en ordre un certain nombre de mots," *PF,* 21). At the same time, literature is something more, namely, an existential project. But it is that project as literature. Neither side can be separated from the other any more than the signifier and signified of a Saussaurian sign. Mallarmé and Kafka are for Blanchot writers whose engagement with writing is not concerned with the relationship to society but with literature. "The writer cannot simply drop out of the game" (*PF,* 22; *WF,* 13)—that very sentence is to be found in Sartre's *Présentation des Temps modernes;*[9] the one that follows, however, is not: "As soon as one starts writing, he is within literature and he is there completely. He is compromised. That is his fate" (*PF,* 22; *WF,* 13).

What does it mean to be "within literature"? First, nothing more than to designate one who works with words. This is no ordinary work, however; rather, it is a compromised one. Writing begins for Blanchot with a catastrophe that robs the self of its possibilities and capabilities—even that of writing. In the beginning of writing is total despair, an existential collapse from which nothing is excepted—not even the possibility of expression. Writing is that paradoxical movement in which the self demurs in the face of its own despair in order to bring it to consciousness. Yet this movement does not proceed as a consciousness that has comprehended itself but rather as the writing down of words and sentences. These express something universal, and in this universality, the particular despair of the self is not retained. That means, however, that the project of expression inverts itself. The self that would come to expression through writing falls, with its own particular suffering, outside of that which is written. Despair is not something that is sublated through the act of writing (i.e., negated, preserved, and raised to a higher state), but rather, it persists. Writing is the paradoxical experience in which the linguistic approach to the matter necessarily falls short, and in so doing, it brings something forth, namely, the work.

In that the self enters literature, it loses itself, since it is entirely handed over to language, and this is no longer its language. Once it existentially steps into literature, there is a neither a return nor an end. For both the extremes of senseless speech and silence are literary expressions. Sense can be ascribed to the former, and the latter can be interpreted. For the writer, there is no longer the possibility of death as there is for Kafka's hunter Gracchus, to which Blanchot always returns. There is no death for him, since there is no life for him other than one in words. But this is a nonlife or an apparent life: "Art is an *as if*" (*PF,* 26; *WF,* 17).

Such a theory of literature rests on a decisive assumption, namely, that authentic (literary) language is not the medium of communication with others but instead the rather imaginary praxis of the solitary self engaging itself. That self is not expressed in language but rather manages its own disappearance through it. Language, as Blanchot avers in reflecting on scattered remarks of Mallarmé, is the movement of negation that knows no sublation of that negation but dissolves it to the extent that language allows the negated to persist:

> *[C]e qu'il [sc. Mallarmé] veut nous révéler comme une chose—et une chose délivrée du hasard—, c'est la tension d'ou naît l'absence, la poursuite sans relâche par laquelle les mots, grâce à leur valeur abstraite, détruisement la matéralité des choses, puis, grâce à leur puissance d'évocation sensible, détruisent cette valeur abstraite, et enfin, par leur mobilité, leur capacité de suspens, tendent de se volatiliser, de s'éteindre eux-mêmes derrière la réciprocité de leurs feux.* (*PF,* 70)

> [W]hat he wants to reveal to us as a thing—and a thing freed from chance—is the tension from which absence is born, the relentless pursuit by which words, thanks to their abstract value, destroy the materiality of things, then, thanks to their evident power of evocation, destroy their abstract value, and finally, by their mobility, their capacity for suspense, try to vanish into thin air to extinguish themselves behind the reciprocity of their fires. (*WF,* 65–66)

With sensitive exactness, Blanchot outlines the aporetic intention that Mallarmé calls poetry. It seeks to make absence something that can be experienced. By virtue of this universality, words, to be sure, destroy the concrete thing, but we are unable to hold onto this absence in everyday language. Since we only perceive the meaning of a word, we again arrive at things. What is required is a renewed approach to the materiality of the word in order to lend duration to the absence of the concrete. The word is no longer the carrier of meaning but rather in its form, as sound and as writing, is itself something material. Once again, we are concerned with something solid that the author is able to dissolve only by placing the word in a constellation with others so that even this materiality, as it were, dissolves. In the movement that ensues, language is released from the function of denotation and meaning and is transformed into a medium of experience—something that Mallarmé himself termed *idée,* by which he could comprehend the presence of something that was essentially absent. That these opposites should cross over to each other is a paradox that fascinated Blanchot.

Blanchot's notion of language can be read as a radicalization of Mallarmé's poetry. If the latter had distinguished between communicative and poetic uses of language, Blanchot questions that difference. Blanchot discovers the focal point of language, even that of everyday speech, in silence, out of which and toward which Mallarmé's poetry unfolds.

> *[C]e vide intérieur, cette contamination des mots par le mutisme et du silence par les mots, désignent peut-être la vérité de toute langue, et particulièrement du langage littéraire, celle que nous recontrerions si nous avions la force d'aller jusqu'au bout, avec la résolution de nous abandonner, rigouresement, méthodiquement, lâchement, au vertige.*[10]

This inner emptiness, this contamination of words through muteness and of silence through words, designates perhaps the truth of each language, and particularly of literary language, of that which we could en-

> counter had we the strength to go to the end, resolved to abandon ourselves rigorously, methodically, cowardly to vertigo.

We are now able to better understand to what extent Blanchot can characterize writing as self-engagement in the mode of irresponsibility. Sartre's sense of engagement is the choice of a political project derived from a determined political historical situation. In a single moment, the self posits its goal, chooses itself, and subordinates the given to that goal. By contrast, Blanchot's sense of engagement is a matter for the solitary self. In language, this self discovers the power of negation, which allows it access to an extreme experience (vertigo) in which the self loses itself.

> *[C]e langage ne suppose personne qui l'exprime, personne qui l'entende: il se* parle *et il s'ecrit. [. . .] Si le langage s'isole de l'homme, comme il isole l'homme de toutes choses, s'il n'est jamais l'acte de quelqu'un qui parle en vue de quelqu'un qui l'entende, on comprendra qu'à celui qui le considère dans cet état de solitude, il offre le spectacle d'une puissance singulière et tout magique. Il est une sorte de conscience sans sujet, qui, séparée de l'être, est détachment, contestation, pouvoir infini de créer le vide et de se situer dans un manque. Mais c'est aussi une conscience incarnée, réduite à la forme matérielle des mots, à leur sonorité, à leur vie et donnant à croire que cette réalité nous ouvre on ne sait quelle voie vers le fond obscur des choses. Peut-être est-ce là une imposture. Mais peut-être cette supercherie est-elle la vérité de toute chose écrite.* (*PF,* 48)

> [T]hat this language does not imply anyone who expresses it, or anyone who hears it: it *speaks* itself and writes *itself.* [. . .] If language isolates itself from man, as it isolates man from everything, if it is never the act of someone who is speaking in the presence of someone who hears him, we come to understand that to one who contemplates it in this state of solitude, it offers the spectacle of a singular and completely magical power. It is a kind of awareness, without subject, that, separated from being, is detachment, questioning, infinite ability to create emptiness and to place itself within loss. But it is also an incarnate consciousness, reduced to the material form of words, to their sonority, their life, and giving us to believe that this reality opens up who knows what path to us into the obscure heart of things. Perhaps that is an imposture. But perhaps trickery is the truth of every written thing. (*WF,* 41–42)

Once again Blanchot is concerned with Mallarmé, but in this passage he simultaneously discusses his own experience. Literature is not, as the romantics would have it, an expression of the self, but essentially of the loss of self: a vertiginous movement that isolates the writer not only from things and other people but also from himself. The limitless power to "create emptiness" and to determine oneself in relation to it corresponds, nonetheless, to the swooning one abandoned by everything real. In *La Littérature et le droit à la mort* (*Literature and the Right to Death*), Blanchot deciphers this power of the writer as one that structurally accords with revolutionary terror: both know only global negation and both do not live their lives but instead their deaths.

Blanchot's theory has the form of a creation myth. In the beginning, the solitary self stands in despair. The only exit that presents itself is writing. At first, the self misconstrues this as a form of expression but soon experiences that it is unable to express its suffering. The suffering remains but falls outside the text, which speaks only of *this* suffering. The same loss overtakes the self: "I have become involved in another in whom, however, I no longer find myself" (*PF,* 29; *WF,* 22). All of its strength is absorbed by what is now its life: that of words, but one in which it cannot find itself. Rather than become conscious of itself in another, the self is lost to a "consciousness without subject"; it is lost to language—an experience that is comparable to death.

The Fury of Disappearance

The experience, we might say, that Blanchot seeks to secure by writing is not a dialectical one. How, then, are we to understand so prominent and central a text such as *La Littérature et le droit à la mort* in which Blanchot explicitly looks to the *Phenomenology of Spirit* for support?[11] One does justice to the Hegelianism of this essay when one understands it as a form of thought that the author engages only the more decisively to distance himself from it. For Blanchot, literature is not a determined negation in which something new emerges from what has been negated, but rather, it is global. Literature negates the world as a totality in order to render it totally at its own disposal—in the imaginary. Since it sets out not to express something definite but rather to grasp the condition for the possibility of language, it does not proceed on the level of a dialectic of subject and object, historical and present time, but instead on the level of being. For Blanchot, and similarly for the author of *Being and Time,* this is accessible only in its inaccessibility. Literature is the paradoxical realization of an undertaking that is completely aporetic.

"The language of literature is a search for this moment which precedes literature. [. . .] it wants the cat as it exists, the pebble taking the side of things, not man but the pebble [. . .]" (*PF,* 316; *WF,* 327). Literature is directed toward a concrete particular, of which Hegel speaks in the *Phenomenology of Spirit,* and while that is our intention, we cannot express that particular, because words always denote a universal. Literature would thus be the attempt to express with the means of language precisely what language necessarily withholds from itself. The hope that this could succeed is based upon the materiality, the "thingness" of words. Acoustically and cursively, the word has a form in which resides for Blanchot (and Mallarmé) the power to conjure things. In that the writer hands himself over to language, it speaks, and the writer disappears behind it; insofar as this disappearance is the writer's, in which the only possibility of the self is achieved, literature is his consciousness. Blanchot grasps the waning presence of the writer in the very act of writing paradoxically: "my consciousness without me" ("ma conscience sans moi"; *PF,* 317).

Just as literary language is simultaneously affirmed and negated as individual consciousness—the self is part of the experience (that is its own) and at the same time is outside of it (it experiences itself in the act of disappearing)—so, in another determination of language, life and death are linked to each other: "the life that bears death and maintains itself in it" (*PF,* 316; *WF,* 327).[12] The sentence can be translated in two ways, depending upon whether death refers to the object or to the subject of speaking. The existence of death includes works, "it brings death" to that which is concrete and preserves itself in death as meaning. At the same time, the existence of words is the death of the one who pronounces them, he disappears in them; from that point on, words are that in which life is preserved.

Blanchot's writing produces an experience through the medium of writing. (That accounts for the strength of his literary critique. Since he exists in literature, experience becomes critique.) The foundation of this experience is solipsism. The bourgeois subject is by himself. The dialectician might insistently reproach the subject that he has deceived himself; the other is necessarily there in relationship to the subject no matter what the subject does. The subject, however, is not to be persuaded that it is anything but alone in its suffering and despair. All talk of the social preconditions of its existence have no effect on this immediate knowledge. It perceives only chatter, nothing that concerns it. If in fact solipsism is an experience, then it is senseless to criticize it, since critique does not address the subject concerning something that it knows immediately about itself. One can, however, attempt to localize it within the field of dialectics. Only if that succeeds (however incompletely) can a history of the solipsistic experience be retrieved. Our real interest is precisely that. What we regard as the alien character of solipsism is merely a sign that we have forgotten it, much as we have forgotten our childhood. And since we must always produce this forgetting anew, we are unable to emerge from the bustle, or what Pascal called *diversion.*

In the history of consciousness that Hegel outlines in the *Phenomenology of Spirit,* the master/slave dialectic occupies a decisive position. Here, consciousness learns that it can behold itself only in and through the other. The subsequent course of consciousness's history takes its cue from the slave who, out of fear of the master, works on things for the master. There is no more talk of the master by Hegel. To be sure, he is recognized following his triumphant battle for prestige, not by his equals but rather by the slave. This recognition, however, means nothing to him. He is alone in the enjoyment of things that the slave has arranged for him. Solipsistic consciousness belongs to the master, that is, to the one who imagines himself to be the master.

The master is alone and yet yearns for recognition. If another arrives and demands to be master, the battle for prestige is repeated. Recognition by another master does not exist. As such, he is occupied with the paradoxical task of recognizing himself. He seeks to be sure of himself as the victor, but the triumph is always a passing one; the figure of the victor pales; it is not the truth of the present. The truth is found only in the here and now, not in memory. In the present, it is the slave who recognizes him. But the slave does not exist as an independent consciousness for him but only as a meager creation who fears his master as a dog does.

The master is alone. He requires another in order to be recognized. Alone, he must generate that other himself. As soon as he appears beside himself as a lucid observer of his despair, he unmasks both figures of the self as playactors. The master needs an angel with whom he can wrestle—an actual one that is not merely a product of his imagination. This angel is language. He does not discover in it a passive medium to reflect his solitude but rather in consciousness without a subject. Once again, he takes to battle (the master can only fight), but the weapons are unevenly divided. He must fight with the weapons of his opponent, who, moreover, has staked out the field of engagement. The master knows that he must lose this fight. He loses the one thing he has: knowledge about the unmistakability of his anguish, which he has returned to himself as something universal. Now, he experiences himself as an embodied contradiction, delivered to a language that robs him of subjectivity. He is no longer to be found in the script that his hand put to paper. Language has made him a traitor to himself. He intended to recognize himself as this traitor and discovers, instead, that he is not self-identical. For the traitor is the one who is not who he is: a living paradox. The world becomes rigidified for him in contradiction.

The other side of the self is the language to which he has sacrificed his despair and person. In this language he negates himself; he can rediscover neither the self nor his suffering in sentences that are in fact his own. And yet he knows himself in them. His life is now one of words. The work is everything to him. But at the same time, it is nothing, an order of words. Reality is negated in its universality (including the reality of the self); universality, by contrast, is negated in its sensory presence. In the space that opens up between both negations, something appears to become visible, something we call truth, but it is only given as something absent.

The Discovery of the Other

In *L'Entretien infini,* a work that blurs the boundary between literary criticism and philosophical discourse, Blanchot's anti-Hegelianism becomes explicit. The conversations in *L'Entretien infini* revolve around the possibility of a nondialectical opposition, of an otherness that would not be negation in the Hegelian sense but rather a radical other without any possible relationship to the self. Precisely in those dialogues in which Blanchot establishes the other as something that has nothing in common with the self, he concedes the validity of the dialectic for the conditions of the interior world ("The dialectical fulfillment is at work, and this is necessary").[13] One detects in these words a type of weak theory that avoids the brusqueness with which Bataille placed expenditure in opposition to the values of productive labor. At first glance, the reason for this astonishing concession regarding the dialectic might be that Blanchot does not want to negate the dialectic, since such a move would situate him on the terrain of the dialectic. He must therefore attempt to circumvent the dialectic by remaining beside, but at the same time without a relationship to, the dialectic and thereby allow for a nondialectical relationship to words. To that end, it does not suffice to posit the particular in opposition to the universal and to halt the movement of sublation; it is much more a question of regarding a lack of commonality as a requirement for human relationship: "[M]y relation with *autrui* is irreducible to any measure, just as it excludes any mediation and any reference to another relation that would include it" (*EI,* 84; *IC,* 59). Where there is no possible level of relationship between the self and the other, the other is the one who threatens me: "[M]an facing man like this has no choice but to speak or to kill" (*EI*, 86; *IC*, 61).

If in fact human relationships are not symmetrical relationships, then the thought suggests itself that they be considered in terms of an acceptance of their radical difference rather than in terms of an acceptance, contrary to all facts, of their similarities. That is what Blanchot does in *L'Entretien infini.* It is a given that Blanchot represents the relationship between master and pupil as one that is determined by an unequal distance of both from each other; for "the master offers nothing to be known that does not remain determined by the indeterminable 'unknown' he represents" (*EI*, 5; *IC*, 6). It is a given that he takes up the asymmetry of the psychoanalytic encounter in which the silence of the analyst allows the patient to recognize himself in his own language (*EI*, 352). As such, he can only represent these situations as nondialectical by overlooking how such actions are goal oriented and by considering them as locked in endless repetition. He thus misses their implicit telos. The relationship between master and pupil makes sense only if the distance that separates them at the outset is overcome so that the pupil himself becomes a master. A true master is one who knows how to make himself superfluous. And even psychoanalytic treatment establishes a goal whereby the patient will no longer require the help of the analyst. In both instances, the conversation that begins ever anew serves the realization of a project; it therefore does not escape the dialectic but moves along inside it.

Apparently, such endless repetition is only to be encountered in empty, everyday conversation, the sort that says neither this nor that but more likely talks everything to death. Blanchot discovers in such speech a subversive force that corrodes all values, even authentic ones. He thus transforms the everyday into the most convincing figure of the *neutre.* Blanchot uses this term to designate the empty site that corresponds to sublation in the dialectic: not synthesis but rather a point of indifference between opposites. To be sure, this movement of thought, which leads Blanchot from Mallarmé's rejection of everyday language as universal reportage to recognition of that language as nondialectical experience, is itself a dialectical movement. Everyday speech, which in contrast to true language is empty chatter, becomes accordingly the truth of language once true language is understood to be empty.

Is there an *authentic speech* for Blanchot? The question is not easy to answer. There is and there is not. Insofar as the nondialectical experience consumes all oppositions, the one between authentic and inauthentic disappears: "the everyday [. . .] ruining always anew the unjustifiable difference between authenticity and inauthenticity" (*EI*, 365; *IC*, 245). On the other hand, the *écriture* of the writer (in the works of the 1940s) is nothing other than a desperate attempt to subject himself to catastrophic experience and to capture that experience in words; in short, an attempt at authenticity. Although Blanchot spent a lifetime of writing circling around the same problem, some relevant shifts in his position can be observed from *Faux pas* to *L'Entretien infini.* In the early writings, the experience of an irreducible solitude provided the starting point for reflection. The self that had fallen into existential crisis necessarily handed itself over to language, in which the self and its particular experience were lost. At the same time, something definite was produced: an analog of its suffering (*PF*, 27). In *L'Entretien infini,* the situation at the outset has changed to the extent that Blanchot begins with the existence of the other, who appears as a stranger with whom the self is in no way connected. Language is thus no longer that of a selfless consciousness radically opposed to the solitary self. Rather, it is the medium that presupposes and maintains the endless distance between mutually estranged subjects: "There is a language because there is nothing in 'common' between those who express themselves: a separation that is presupposed—not surmounted, but confirmed—in all true speech" (*EI*, 79; *IC*, 55). The (absolute) difference that separates the self from the other is not to be overcome but rather something that must be maintained even in linguistic communication.

> *Parler à quelqu'un [. . .] c'est le reconnaître inconnu et l'accueillir étranger, sans l'obliger à rompre sa différence. En ce sens, la parole est la terre promis où l'exil s'accomplit en séjour, puisqu'il ne s'agit pas d'y être chez soi, mais toujours au Dehors, en un mouvement où l'Etranger se délivre sans se renoncer.* (*EI*, 187)

> To speak to someone [. . .] is to recognize him as unknown and to receive him as foreign without obliging him to break with his difference. Speech, in this sense, is the promised land where exile fulfills itself in sojourn since it is not a matter of being at home there but of being always Outside, engaged in a movement wherein the Foreign offers itself yet without disavowing itself. (*IC*, 128)

Language is no longer the angel with whom the solitary self wrestles, but rather the promised land (*das versprochene Land*) in which it is permitted to live without that land ever becoming one's own—a site of recognition that grants the other its strangeness. Opposed to these sentences, which in some fashion are the outlines of a hermeneutic lacking only a horizon of convergence, are clearly others that consider the distance between strangers as hierarchically structured. "As *Autrui* is the Master, all true speech is magisterial," he reflects in a dialogue that fondly moves in the direction of Lévinas (*EI*, 80; *IC*, 56). The self of *vraie parole* (true speech) would be no self but rather the other. To speak is always to take up the position of the master, to place oneself in an endless distance from any possible listeners, to make oneself unknown to them but also to transform oneself into the other. If one asks, who then is the master, Blanchot's texts answer with echoes of the sentences cited earlier. The master is the one capable of *vraie parole*. One could perhaps also say that the master is the one who can articulate an affirmation that would be not the negation of a negation, but rather a pure positing requiring no justification and whose word carried authority (I refer to Blanchot's explanation of Bataille's experience of the limit; *EI*, 316). And yet we read in the same chapter sentences about the true speech that seem to point in an entirely different direction: "[S]peaking is our fortune, our chance, and to speak is to go in search of chance, the chance of a relation 'immediately' without measure" (*EI*, 314; *IC*, 211–12). In one instance, the endless distance that lends the world of the master a nonderivable authority; in the other articulation, the search for a relationship with the other in which proximity and distance cross. These are contradictions but are not presented as such in Blanchot's thought, since it is grounded, after all, in the indifference of opposites.

Lordship, according to a conclusion of Kojève's Hegel interpretation, is "an existential dead end. The master can either become stultified in pleasure or die as the master on the battlefield, but he cannot live consciously and know himself to be content by virtue of what he is."[14] Blanchot is among those who do not allow this verdict to prevent them from entering that blind alley and seeking an exit.

> One can hope that these texts will be *deformed* by the new way of looking at them that others bring to them.
>
> —Roland Barthes, Avant-propos to *Critical Essays*

5. Roland Barthes, Writer

In the autobiographical book of aphorisms *Roland Barthes,* one finds in a text entitled "L'Exclusion" the exclusion. In the third person (a translation back from the autobiographical "I" to a "he"), Barthes reports of an actual feeling of exclusion that took hold of him as he happened to witness a wedding while passing through the church of Saint-Sulpice. He adds a reflection that clarifies the intensity of the thought.

> *Car aux exclusions simples que cet épisode lui représentait, s'ajoutait un dernier éloignement: celui de son langage: il ne pouvait assumer son trouble dans le code même du trouble, c'est-à-dire* l'exprimer: *il se sentait plus qu'exclu:* détaché: *toujours renvoyé à la place du* témoin. (*RB,* 89)

> For to the simple exclusions which this episode represented for him was added a final alienation; that of his language: he could not assume his distress in the very code of distress, i.e., *express it:* he felt more than excluded: *detached:* forever assigned the place of the *witness.* (*Eng.,* 86)

The scene can be interpreted as the dissolve of two scenes. In the first of these, he whom with reservation we might call R. B., experiences himself as one incapable of participating in life, and in the second, he learns that he is denied immediate expression of this sorrow. In both scenes, Barthes is a witness. He is witness to an event whose significance is maintained only because he is not a participant. The wedding does not touch him but only his state of exclusion. In response to this experience, he assumes the role of the observer. He is not in accord with the actual experience. It is there but as something that does not belong to him. He experiences himself as someone who cannot have experience but can only look back at those who do (and that would be this R. B.). To be sure, the witness can offer a report of what he has seen, but he is unable to express that from the perspective of one who has lived it. The one writing never articulates himself in the text. There is no expression, only the longing for it.

The text betrays a romantic disposition. The experiences that he reports make sense only if one starts with an identical subject that, as always, is subordinated to temporality and in conflict with itself. Only as such can it experience itself as excluded and long for the immediacy of linguistic expression. The text gets around this presupposition by grounding the identity in its own lack of accord with actual experiences. In the aphorism that follows "L'Exclusion," Barthes speaks of the "inconsistency of the subject" and the privation of immediate expression. Similar to the one from life, that of language also refers to a lack that becomes an object of longing: Can longing, to ask along with Lukács, bring about a form?

Longing is the intensive experience of a lack. Its object (life) is right in front of the eyes of the observer, but it is not given to him. Something separates him from it, and that something is interwoven with him in a manner that is not entirely transparent. If longing is not already stilled, then it must be spoken. But in order to utter it, the words must come from the heart and not the lexicon. So, a longing for expression arises from the longing for life. The writer, Barthes remarks in *Critique et vérité,* internally maintains the belief that the sign is not arbitrary and that the name is a natural property of the thing. ("Fundamentally, the writer always nurtures the belief that signs are not arbitrary and that the name is a natural property of the thing" *CV,* 52; *CT,* 69). And one must add: He knows that the signs of language are arbitrary. His task is to posit arbitrary linguistic signs as if they were natural; that is, to produce symbols.

Wherever the immediacy of linguistic expression is disguised, the disguise offers only the chance of happening upon something like immediacy. The path to the proper (necessary) expression is paradoxically through imitation. This is not primarily one of linguistic expression; it is rather directed toward demeanor, the *posture* of the writer: Gide traveling, reading the classics and taking *notes.*

> *Cette façon de se promener dans le monde, un carnet dans la poche et une phrase dans la tête (tel je voyais Gide circulant de la Russie au Congo, lisant ses classiques et écrivant ses carnets au wagon-restaurant en attendant les*

plats; tel je vis réellement, un jour de 1939, au fond de la brasserie Lutétia, mangeant une poire et lisant un livre). (*RB,* 81)

> His way of strolling through the world, a notebook in his pocket and a phrase in his head (the way I imagined Gide traveling from Russia to the Congo, reading his classics and writing his notebooks in the dining car, waiting for the meals to be served; the way I actually saw him, one day in 1939, in the gloom of the Brasserie Lutétia, eating a pear and reading a book). (*Eng.,* 77, 79)

Gide's *posture* therefore becomes an object of desire, because it is the natural sign for "writer." Gide, as he loves and lives, *is* the writer, both in his concrete individuality and in his embodiment of the universal concept. He is, in short, a living symbol. Barthes discovers the naturalness of the sign that R. B. searches for in vain in language embodied in the writer Gide, and Barthes nestles up to the object of desire. Imitation, so he hopes, will transform him into the one he longs to be: one who is the proper expression of a powerful writer. But what appears to him as nature, as embodied meaning, is in truth a role, in which the sign and the signified are not quite congruent.

> *On copie un rôle [. . .]: je commence à produire en reproduisant celui que je voudrais être.* (*RB,* 103)

> One copies a role [. . .]: I begin producing by reproducing the person I want to be. (*Eng.,* 99)

Even worse, it is a matter of a cliché. In *Mythologies,* he subjects it to critique:

> *Gide lisait du Bossuet en descendant le Congo. Cette posture résume assez bien l'ideal de nos écrivain "en vacances," photographiés par le* Figaro: *joindre au loisir banal le prestige d'une vocation que rien ne peut arrêter ni dégrader. Violà donc un bon reportage, bien efficace sociologiquement, et qui nous renseigne sans tricher sur l'idee que notre bourgeoisie se fait des ses écrivains.* (*M,* 29)

> Gide was reading Bossuet while going down the Congo. This posture sums up rather well the ideal of our writers "on holiday," as photographed by *Le Figaro:* to add to mere leisure the prestige of a vocation which nothing can stop or degrade. Here is therefore a good piece of journalism, highly efficient sociologically, and which gives us, with-

out cheating, information on the idea which our bourgeoisie entertains about its writers. (*Eng.*, 29)

The image is the same—Gide traveling as the "in" image of the writer—but the analysis points in another direction. If the autobiographical fragment, although it blends the experience of the young R. B. with a critical attitude, represented the phantasm of the writer as the driving force of the imagination, the text from *Mythologies* is concerned with the destruction of the naturalness of the image, which had formerly constituted its fascination for R. B.

Barthes, the critic of ideology, uses the image to construct two mutually contradictory messages: namely, (1) the writer is a person like you and me (he takes vacations like everyone else), and (2) the writer is an exceptional person (he works even on vacation). What appears to be primarily a demystification of the writer functions in truth as a means to intensify that mystification. The uniqueness of his "vocation" is emphasized by the prosaic circumstances of its appearance. Barthes calls the image of "writer on holiday" mythic because it transforms history into nature. Both the social actuality, "vacation," and the idea of an inspired artist are historical. This historicity is erased in the image through the obviousness with which its meaning is extended to the analytically unschooled observer. This observer deciphers the image not as a sign that transmits a message but rather as something meaningful in itself, as an inseparable unity of nature and meaning. Stated otherwise, myth is a sign that in large measure is justified: "une parole *excessivement* justifiée" (*M*, 238).

If our analysis is correct, then the young R. B.'s object of longing, of which the autobiographical fragments speak, and the object of critique in *Mythologies* are the same: the justified sign and the immediate expression. There would be in Barthes's thinking/writing a point in which the opposition of values collapses. The object of desire and the falsehood that the critical discourse unmasks would be one and the same. They are and they are not. To be sure, the desired immediacy of expression returns as something false in myth, but it does not simply coincide with myth. The immediacy that claims to be a given is false, but the same is not the case in longing. Only as something absent and something given in appearance is immediacy justified.

In retrospect, we have interpreted Barthes's autobiographical texts as a rendering of experience with the knowledge that for us the experience is only textual. This allows the subject to recognize that certainty is given as something excluded from life and the immediacy of expression. The first exclusion concerns R. B.'s individuality, which it constructs; he shares the second with all others. The writer does believe in the possibility of a language of names in which the names are a natural attribute of things, but he also knows that linguistic signs are arbitrary. Wherever (in modernity) the justified sign shows itself to be a given, it turns out to be an untruth, a false nature. It is justified only as a horizon of longing. Is longing capable, we asked ourselves, of bringing about a form? Barthes speaks of exclusion without noting from what the subject is excluded. We said, it is excluded from life, but that is only an auxiliary concept that lends, at best, that which is not determined the appearance of certainty. Since one who longs knows life only as something denied him, he is in need of a different object. He finds it in the artwork. He becomes a critic, assuming the role that has devolved to him—of witness. Now, he is far removed from his goal of proper form. Longing is without form; it is a blurring of contours. Therefore, Barthes must counter that with a strictness of form. How does the critic become a writer?

"Si J'Etais Écrivain, et Mort"

What is a critic? The answer appears to be simple. It could be something like the following: an author who writes about the literary work of others with the intention to grasp them interpretively and answer them authentically. But does that apply to the critic Roland Barthes? Does he not more likely write, as Georg Lukács says of the essayist, "on the occasion of . . ." (*bei Gelegenheit von . . .*)? The works that he comments upon would then be his object but not what he is concerned about in his writing. "The critic is a writer" is stated quite precisely in the preface to *Essais critiques* (*EC*, 9). But it is precisely the pregnant brevity of this formulation that raises problems. It questions a boundary that we presume is obvious when we talk about literary criticism—the one between a literary text and literary criticism. Barthes's thought is simple: The medium of the critic, like that of the writer, is language; therefore, he cannot reveal the hidden truth of a work but rather cover it with language:

> *La "preuve" critique, si elle existe, dépend d'une aptitude, non à* decouvrir *l'oeuvre interrogée, mais au contraire à la* couvrir *le plus complètement possible par son propre langage.* (*EC*, 256)

> Critical "proof," if it exists, depends on an aptitude not to *discover* the work in question but on the contrary to *cover* it as completely as possible by its own language. (*CE*, 259)

That is clearly a provocation. The critic, that is to say the interpreter, no longer makes himself disappear by bringing up the text under consideration, but rather covers it up with his own speech. In Barthes's literary critical essays, this speech has a dual form (although they certainly often overlap one another): the one as a structuralist (scientific) discourse of the rules and constraints to which the text's production of meaning is subjected; the other as its own literary speech that extends the metaphors of the text. There would thus be two ways to connect to a literary text: the metonymic, which addresses what is adjacent to the textual, and the metaphorical, which transports it. But is the critic really the writer? Does not the very exclusion from life's immediacy, what one could call by way of Lukács the a priori of experience, separate him from the writer? There is a text by Barthes in which he attempts with linguistic means to tackle that question; that is (for him), to get around it.

> *Car s'il faut que par une dialectique retorse il y ait dans le Texte, destructeur de tout sujet, un sujet à aimer, ce sujet est dispersé, un peu comme les cendres que l'on jette au vent après la mort (au thème de l'urne et de la stèle, objets forts, fermés, instituteurs du destin, s'opposeraient les éclats du souvenir, l'erosion qui ne laisse de la vie passée que quelques plis): si j'etais écrivain, et mort, comme j'aimerais que ma vie se réduisît, par les soins d'un biographe amical et désinvolte, à quelques détails, à quelques goûts, à quelques inflexions, disons: des "biographèmes," dont la distinction et la mobilité pourraient voyager hors de tout destin et venir toucher, à la façon des atomes épicuriens, quelque corps futur, promis à la même dispersion; une vie trouée, en somme, comme Proust a su écrire la sienne dans son oeuvre, ou encore un film, à l'ancienne manière, duquel toute parole est absente et dont le flot d'images (ce* flumen orationis *en quoi consiste peut-être la "cochonnerie" de l'écriture) est entrecoupé, à la façon de hoquets salutaires, par le noir à peine écrit de l'intertitre, l'irruption désinvolte d'un* autre *signifiant.* (*SFL*, 14)
>
> For if, through a twisted dialectic, the Text, destroyer of all subject, contains a subject to love, that subject is dispersed, somewhat like the ashes we strew into the wind after death (the theme of the urn and the stone, strong closed objects, instructors of fate, will be contrasted with the

> bursts of memory, the erosion that leaves nothing but a few furrows of past life): were I a writer, and dead, how I would love it if my life, through the pains of some friendly and detached biographer, were to reduce itself to a few details, a few preferences, a few inflections, let us say: to "biographemes" whose distinction and mobility might go beyond any fate and come to touch, like Epicurean atoms, some future body, destined to the same dispersion; a marked life, in sum, as Proust succeeded in writing his in his work, or even a film, in the old style, in which there is no dialogue and the flow of images (that *flumen orationis* which perhaps is what makes up the "obscenities" of writing) is intercut, like the relief of hiccoughs, by the barely written darkness of the intertitles, the casual eruption of *another* signifier. (*Eng.*, 8–9)

With cheerful seriousness the text plays around with Blanchot's theme of writing and death. Insofar as the one writing must submit himself to language, the text destroys the subject; at the same time, it produces a subjectivity that only shares as much with the one writing as do the ashes of the deceased with the living being who those ashes once were. Its status is metaphorical: subject-ashes. And in the exact sentences that speak of the subject, Barthes pronounces, "I," and he imagines this "I" as dead, thus placing the necessary death of the subject (the author is always dead as the one who has written the text) and the imaginary death of his own self in an analogical relationship that is not easily unraveled: particles of subjectivity (subject-ashes, "Biographeme") remain of both. The possibility of an expressive subject is simultaneously thrown into question and maintained. To stay with the image, in the text the subject is burning but holds onto itself as something fragmented.

"Were I a writer, and dead"—the sentence instantiates a dialectic that turns back on itself in ever more complicated fashion. What from all appearances is a clear statement ("I, R. B., am no writer and certainly not a dead one") is mirrored in its opposite by the fact that the sentence is clearly marked as a literary one. (It does not read, "were I a dead writer," but rather, "were I a writer, and dead.") The sentence unmistakably says, "I am the sentence of a writer." The same movement of insetting incompatibles immediately follows: Proust, the writer, could transpose the fragments of his life into his work. We could add, "I, R. B., who is no writer, cannot do this."[1] Even this (indirect) statement is contradicted by the chain of comparisons recalling Proust that follows: "like Proust [. . .] or even a film [. . .] in the fashion of healthy hiccups."[2]

Can the entanglement to which Barthes has brought us (or to which we have brought Barthes's text) be unraveled? Barthes is not a writer (like Proust), he has no work. But he writes, and in so doing becomes what he is not: a writer. The movement of the text, which curiously circles around itself, does not leave the concept of the writer untouched. On the one hand, he is the person who writes; at the same time, however, he is the one who does not write, who cannot write (once again, we are reminded of Blanchot). What he writes is never actual writing or the production of a work, but rather something that forever defers such writing until it shows itself as a work—*post festum* and for others. The completed work would be the death of the author; therefore, he can never write it. Insofar as the essayist writes without ever achieving the work, he is the modern writer par excellence. Unlike the novelist, he knows that there is no modern masterpiece: "A modern masterpiece is impossible" (*DZ,* 63; *WDZ,* 86).

Can the longing for a work bestow a form? There must be a form that molds the indifference point of possible opposites, in which death is the object of desire, play is mixed with earnestness, and lofty artistic speech appears as unmediated. For Barthes, this form is the maxim: "elle est essentiellement un discours ambigu, situé à la frontière de deux mondes [. . .]: celui de la mort et celui du jeu" (*NEC,* 87; "it is essentially an ambiguous discourse, located at the frontier of two worlds [. . .]: that of death and that of play"; *NCE,* 21).

"Ces Oppositions Sont des Artefacts"

"I write classic" reads the wholly unclassical final sentence of an aphorism, in which Barthes renders an account of how he writes (*RB,* 95; *Eng.,* 92). Where does the self-proclaimed classicism of his manner of writing lie? First of all, in the decision for clear and simple sentence construction, second, in the preference for abbreviated formulations to the point of paradox (*to detach* is the essential gesture of classical art; *RB,* 72; *Eng.,* 68), and finally, in the structuring function that conceptual opposites assume in his texts, whether they be taken from scientific language (denotation/connotation, signifier/signified) or whether he creates them himself (*écrivains/écrivants, écriture/style*). We might take a closer look at them since they perhaps most readily allow for identification of what might be called his mode of thought.

Striking about Barthes's conceptual opposites is, first of all, that they do not serve as neutral instruments of analysis but are almost always over-determined through a juxtaposition of values.[3] By contrasting *écrivains* and *écrivants* in an essay of the same name, Barthes in no way describes two mutually opposed types of writers, the producer of literature and the engaged intellectual; rather, he combines opposing values, which, in turn, afford him the opportunity to break with Sartre's concept of engagement. To that end, he develops two different linguistic strategies. Either he assumes Sartre's concepts but lends them an alternative semantic content by defining them in an immanently literary sense, such as *to engage oneself* and *to be responsible* (*DZ*, 14; *EC*, 150); or, he proceeds in the opposite manner, skewers the concept of *s'engager* (using it this time in Sartre's sense of the word) in order finally to define literature as *a wanting engagement* (*EC*, 150). As stated, these techniques of semantic reassignment serve in the aforementioned essay to break with Sartre's type of intellectual, with the *écrivant*. Even more surprising is the article's conclusion, in which the opposition of *écrivain* and *écrivant* is not sublated into some form of synthesis but rather blurred by the remark that every intellectual who writes is subjected today (i.e., 1941) to both demands: to write something (*écrivant*) and to write (*écrivain*).

The concluding characterization of *écrivain-écrivant* supports the notion that Barthes is concerned with the actual gesture of blurring opposites. Since the society in question simultaneously recognizes him and keeps him at a distance, he could be said to be integrated by virtue of his exclusion: "an excluded figure integrated by his very exclusion, a remote descendant of the accursed" (*EC*, 154; *CE*, 150). The dialectical formulation is deceptive. Barthes does not think of the state of exclusion as a means to connect with the other, but rather as a blurring of opposites: the *écrivain-écrivant* is both excluded and integrated. In this instance, the motif in his thought of a third term does not suggest, as it does in later texts, an unreachable horizon but rather the bad reality of compromise.

The process of blurring opposites, which was developed earlier, is also found, albeit less noticeably, in other writings. In *Le Degré zéro de l'ecriture*, his first publication to attract a lot of attention, Barthes devotes considerable energy to lending a new contour to the concept of *écriture* by placing it always anew in opposition to something (among others, *style* and *parole*). The numerous determinations that follow as a result suggest exactness or at least an effort toward it. But if the reader tries to understand them, he is soon lost in a jungle of concepts and images. The reader, nonetheless, has the impression that Barthes is describing something with *écriture* that previously has never been seen. He also orients himself according to pregnant definitions such as the following: "Writing is thus essentially the morality of form" (*DZ,* 15; *WDZ,* 15). And he will note the almost corporeal concept of style that is sharply distinguished from that of *écriture* ("It is the product of a thrust not of an intention"; *DZ,* 12; *WDZ,* 11). To be sure, toward the end of the study, Barthes abandons the opposition. What until now he had called *degré zéro de l'écriture* is now discussed as the "search for a non style or an oral style" (*DZ,* 64; *WDZ,* 87). In light of what we can observe from other essays, one cannot simply read carelessness into it, but rather the first formulation of a principle. Barthes does not want to introduce a new term into literary criticism. He knows the oppositions that he has developed are artificial constructions—"such oppositions are artefacts" (*RB,* 96; *Eng.,* 92)—and he wants to make their artificiality visible. The critic's morals are those of the honest card player who puts his cards on the table. The opposition introduced at the beginning of the text between style and *écriture* has given rise to a reflection (or is it simply a gesture of writing?) that in the end returns to a traditional concept of style. The construction of such an opposition may collapse, but the result is not simply a zero-sum game. The imploding construction produces an insight which otherwise could not have been won.

The imprecise concept, *écriture,* which means a historically determined literary problematic of form and, at the same time, the principle underlying the individual choice of the author that molds style, enables him to grasp simultaneously from within and without the situation of the modern writer. In the aftermath of the (failed) revolution of 1848, in which class antagonisms became apparent, the unified *écriture classique* collapsed along with the bourgeois ideology of the essence of man (Barthes speaks of "an essentialist mythology of man"; *DZ,* 43; *WDZ,* 58). Since writers have turned away from the bourgeoisie, which, nevertheless, determines their living situation, the literary style breaks apart. As a result, there is a problematic of form, which consists in the fact that every literary text that speaks about itself formulates a position opposed to literature as an institution. Literature becomes a secondary system of markings that refer to each other. Insofar as the modern writer cannot dodge the system (every design for an antiliterary style receives via the institution the mark of the literary), he is excluded from living (spoken) language. In modern writing, the unconditional responsibility of the author for the style he has chosen (Barthes speaks of an "ethic of writing," *DZ,* 62; *WDZ,* 84) is imbricated in a historically imposed problem of form for which he is not responsible ("dont il n'est pas responsable"; *DZ,* 63). Insofar as Barthes uses the same concept to grasp the individual choice of style and the historical problem of form, the opposition between responsibility and nonresponsibility collapses. At the same time, the exclusion from unmediated expression, which surfaced as experience in the autobiographical fragment R. B., can be understood as the fate of the modern writer and thus deindividualized.

Barthes knows a lot about the writer Roland Barthes. An aphorism from the "autobiography" describes precisely his conversancy with oppositional pairs. He concludes with the following remark:

> *[M]on text est en effet* lisible: *je suis du côte de la structure, de la phrase, du texte phrasé: je produis pour reproduire, comme si j'avais une pensée et que je la représente à l'aide de matériaux et de règles:* j'écris classique. (*RB,* 96)

> [M]y test is in fact *readerly:* I am on the side of structures, of the sentence, of the sentenced text: I produce in order to reproduce, as if I had a thought and represent it with the help of raw materials and of rule: *I write classic.* (*Eng.,* 92)

The text in which Barthes asserts the readability of his own texts is oddly ambiguous. Their supposed readability is owed, above all, to the pairs of oppositions that construct a structure. But the attendant obligations are not settled ("The opposition is *minted* [like a coin] but one does not seek to *honor* it"; *Eng.,* 92). The readable text is a blurred text. "As if I had a thought"—a thought anterior to linguistic formulation? But already in *Le Degré zéro de l'écriture* it is stated: There is no thought without language ("il n'y a pas de pensée sans langage"; *DZ,* 61; *WDZ,* 83). The reproduction of a prelinguistic thought is the pretense that the production of linguistic thought assumes in Barthes: Because I have no thoughts, I can produce them in that I act as if I reproduce a thought that I do (not) have. The oppositional structures are instruments for the production of thought that issues from writing: thoughts of writing/writing of thoughts. "J'écris classique." The sentence—and this is seldom the case with Barthes—is grammatically deviant. It is fashioned after the model, "Je parle français." *Écriture classique* is treated like a language. Through grammatical deviation, the sentence simultaneously says the opposite of what it pronounces.

Barthes's classicism is unclassical. Something from early German romanticism returns, which Barthes could hardly have known:

> *dès le départ, aucune volonté de sens général, aucune envie d'assumer un "destin" intellectuel: seulement les éclats d'un travail progressif, souvent obscur à lui-même.* (*EC4,* 8)

From the beginning no will to universal meaning, no desire to assume an intellectual destiny; only the splinter of a progressive work, which is often obscured even for him.

So Barthes remarks in 1971 about the new edition of his earlier *Essais critiques,* whose arrangement he characterized as rhapsodic (a word treasured by Friedrich Schlegel). It is not a matter of a synthesis of classical form and romantic content but rather of the structural principles of a prose schooled in Gide and Valéry that turns into its opposite. Certainly, there is always the countermovement in Barthes that brings the playful back into a discourse of instruction.

Almost pedantically, he

gives precise meaning to the intended meaning of a word: "the word 'proposition' must be understood here in a sense more grammatical than logical" (*EC4,* 70)
points out a wordplay: "today the critic alone executes the work (I allow word play)" (*EC4,* 76)
explains an equivocal term: " 'development' (a word significantly ambiguous: biologically and rhetorically)" (*EC4,* 74)

Le texte lui-même joue *(comme une porte, comme un appareil dans lequel il y a du "jeu"); le lecteur joue, lui, deux fois: il joue* au *Texte (sens ludique) [. . .], il* joue le *Texte; il ne faut pas oublier que "jouer" est aussi un terme musical.* (*EC4,* 76)

The text itself plays (like a door, like a device loosely mounted that has "room to play"); the reader plays in a double sense: he plays the text [as one plays a musical instrument], and [. . .] he plays it [like a score]; one should not forget that "to play" is also a musical term.

Taken from a single essay, the examples attest to the density in applying the process. By amassing equivocal terms, or more precisely, through articulation of their equivocity in the text, the process is revealed to be a literary one that plays with words (see *RB,* 76f). Since the author pronounces as effect the literary effect produced by him, he destroys its effect. Once again, Barthes turns this destruction of the desired effect into a principle that shapes his text. The text is constructed from stringing together the destroyed effects and thus producing an effect to the second power. The process recalls Brecht's estrangement effect, without actually copying it. Beneath the surface, it is probably due to a poorly suppressed dialectic of desire. The literary expression is the object of desire, and, at the same time, it is forbidden. The found (actualized) ambiguity is the fulfillment of the desire for expression, if only directly so. This fulfillment is forfeited to moral critique: the desired ambivalence is at the same time what is reprehensible. It must therefore be defused in that one makes it explicit. But insidiously, desire asserts itself anew by making a process out of the destruction of the effect.

Can longing bring about a form? So our question read. It can. The form carries a name: essay. The object of longing is the unmediated linguistic expression, that is, writing that coincides with living. As a picture of reality, this unity is mystical. History is transformed into nature; as phantasm, it is the driving force of an activity that reaches its target by constantly missing it. The role of the critic, as does that of the scientist, seems to presume a renunciation of the literary work, but the appearance is deceptive. The critic not only has language as his object, but it is also the medium in which he moves. To the extent that he understands his activity as writing, he becomes a writer. Concepts turn up in his texts like allegorical figures. They have as little permanence as such figures. But from the trace of ash that these figures leave behind, we read the absent thoughts of the author and the traits of a living subject.

For Malte Fues, to whom this essay is indebted

6. Thought as Gesture

Michel Foucault, Philosopher

Morbus Hermeneuticus

Philosophers, so one reads, are afflicted by an illness, *morbus hermeneuticus*. Instead of pursuing philosophy, they read and interpret philosophical texts and successfully pass this activity off as philosophy. Interpretation is recognized as philosophical achievement, "even when a philosophical thought of the interpreter himself is not to be found." The diagnostician of the new illness is incensed: "Philosophy seeks to move ahead as literary science."[1] To him, literary critics are apparently people who not only do not think but also cannot be expected to think. But what does it mean to think? What is a philosophical thought? Robert Musil, a writer and thus someone who, at any rate, is not expected to think but who is under the suspicion of having thought, has presented a less than flattering description of thought and compared it to a blockage that will not come loose. Perhaps it was not philosophical thought that Musil was talking about. Be that as it may, I fear, it is by and large to be conceded the diagnostician that most literary critics do not think. If he is correct that philosophers today do not think, wherein then lies the difference between philosophers and nonphilosophers?

The quarrel is illuminating because it shows that following what the history of philosophy calls the collapse of the Hegelian system, philosophy has not become so modest as to understand itself as one science alongside other sciences. The quarrel certainly concerns the cultural power of the discipline, but beyond that it is a question of whether there is still something that deserves the name of philosophy. With that, we have arrived at our topic.

Is Michel Foucault a Philosopher?

Undoubtedly, answers Gilles Deleuze, his work stands alongside those great philosophical works that have altered the concept of thinking. "Foucault's work re-connects with the great works that have changed what it means for us to think."[2]

Specifically, he argues, Foucault discovered a philosophical object, the *énoncé* (the statement, "Aussage") that coincides neither with the word nor with the grammatical or logical sentence, but rather penetrates these like a diagonal. Beginning with the *Archéologie du savoir,* Deleuze tries to demonstrate the unity of Foucaldian thinking by conceiving of *statements* and *visibilités* as a priori conditions of real experience. In this sense, he speaks of a "neo-Kantianism proper to Foucault."[3] Foucault himself had viewed this somewhat differently. More likely, he wanted "to remove the transcendental prop" ("lever la butée transcendentale"; *AS,* 148). Foucault indicates that his efforts aim to free the history of thought from its subjection to the transcendental ("affranchir l'histoire de la pénsée de la sujétion transcendentale"; *AS,* 264). Apparently, Deleuze is concerned with inserting Foucault into the history of Western philosophy. To that end, a series of operations is required. It must be shown that the author has discovered a new object (the *énoncé*), that in doing so he provided a new answer to the great questions in the history of philosophy (Foucault as an innovator in transcendental philosophy), and finally, that his thought forms a unity. In order to represent the philosopher Foucault, his texts must be subjected precisely to those procedures that they argue against: specifically, interpretation from the perspective of originality and the continuation of a tradition in which the function of the author is a medium to bestow form.[4]

To avoid any misunderstanding, I am not criticizing Deleuze but rather trying to find out what he is doing. Foucault proposes and practices an intercourse with texts that he calls *discourse analysis* and whose particularity leads the gaze to the conditions at the margins according to which texts are produced. He combined his theory of discourse with a polemic against interpretation. However one stands in relationship to this polemic, Deleuze ignores that polemic as well as the practice of discourse analysis. He writes an interpretation. The representation of Foucault as a great philosopher negates (unwillingly) Foucault's work.

Even Manfred Frank places a patient reconstruction of what Foucault terms *énoncé* in the middle of his Foucault chapter in his lectures on neostructuralism. He thereby arrives at the following conclusion: Either *énoncé* is an individual linguistic utterance, in which case it would only be accessible via a divinatory hermeneutic (which, in any case is rejected by Foucault), or it is subjected in some fashion to undetermined discursive rules and is thus decipherable according to a master code. Foucault, however, would link both points of view: "the unforseeability of the effects of meaning" and "the thought of order." The result is a hybrid construction that recalls the weak clocks of Dali's painting, which, likewise, have no correspondence to reality.[5] A severe formulation ensues in which Frank, in anticipation of the analysis, summarily condemns Foucault's effort: "It does not inaugurate a new kind of thinking but more likely is the back stairs to that what we have already known and whose return we should not unconditionally wish."[6]

The sentence from Deleuze cited earlier, in which he situates Foucault among the great philosophers of the West, reads as a response to Frank. We are on the German-French playing field for the championship of European philosophy. I will not try to assume the role of umpire, particularly since I suspect that something is amiss with the rules of the game. If one asks the question whether Foucault inaugurates a new kind of thinking (Frank as well as Deleuze poses this question), then there is just as little reason for considering unity and freedom from contradiction as self-evident criteria as there is for considering the ability of a theory to explain the conditions of its possibility as a criterion. In other words, I have the suspicion that Frank and Deleuze enumerate the question of whether it is a new kind of thinking with Foucault from within a philosophical understanding that Foucault's thinking especially puts into question.

Methodological Interjections

> Your archaeology is not a science.
>
> —Foucault on Foucault, *AS*, 268; *AK*, 206

There are ways to engage Foucault without reconstructing his philosophical thought. But they are subject as well to the Foucauldian critique of interpretation. Commentary or interpretation (Foucault does not differentiate between the two genres) pursues a contradictory writing project: It should simultaneously say something new and thereby say only that which the text to be commented upon actually says. The ideal commentary would then be that which Borges devised for *Don Quixote,* one that repeats the text verbatim.

> *D'une part il [sc. le commentaire] permet de construire (et indéfiniment) des discours nouveaux [. . .]. Mais, d'autre part, le commentaire n'a pour rôle, quelles que soient les techniques mises en oeuvre, que de dire* enfin *ce qui était articulé silencieusement là-bas. Il doit, selon un paradoxe qu'il déplace tourjours mais auquel il n'échappe jamais, dire pour la première fois ce qui cependant avait été déjà dit et répéter inlassablement ce qui pourtant n'avait jamais été dit.* (*OD,* 27)

> On the one hand, it [commentary] permits us to create new discourses [. . .]. On the other hand, whatever the techniques employed, commentary's only role is to say *finally,* what has silently been articulated *deep down.* It must—and the paradox is ever-changing yet inescapable—say, for the first time, what has already been said, and repeat tirelessly what was, nevertheless, never said. ("OD," 221)

The critique of the commentator rests on two unspoken assumptions: (1) Commentary and the text to be commented upon reside in a relationship of ideal simultaneity with each other, and (2) The commentator negates himself as a historically determined subject in the commentary since he only says what the text says. If one does not share both presuppositions, if one presumes in the sense of a critical hermeneutic that the distance separating commentary from the text to be commented upon is always historical and that the commentator maintains himself as a historically determined subject in commenting on texts from the past so as to recognize his own presence in the process, then it seems that the practice of commenting on texts from the past is in no way the sort of paradox that Foucault represents.

One can respond with Foucault, however, even if one grants the validity of this charge, that commentary remains a unique effort to reclaim a deep dimension from the text, to pronounce the meaning that the text holds without pronouncing it. One could answer that since Schleiermacher, hermeneutics has legitimated its claim to understand the text better than the author. Stated otherwise, the question about the meaning of a text is not directed toward the author's intended meaning (also not—if one might so remark—toward the unconscious intended meaning) but rather toward the possible falling into meaning of the text through different contextualizations (the manner in which a text acquires meaning through various contextualizations). The "depth" of a text is an appearance produced linguistically through semantic ambiguity and culturally through canonization; it is something we need in order to be able to understand ourselves (through the mediation of texts). When one poses the question about the meaning of a text in a fashion that it becomes no longer a question about hidden meaning but rather one about the means of contextualization, then the opposition of meaning and discourse analysis loses its precision; for discourse analysis is nothing other than a means of contextualizing texts.

With this remark, the difference between the question about the rules and mechanisms of control to which a discourse is subjected and the question about the meaning of a text should not be leveled, although the appearance of their unconnectability is made recognizable. Discourse analysis relies on hermeneutics without simply being taken up by it. The question about the manner in which discursive marginal conditions form the concrete text assumes an understanding of the text that follows hermeneutic principles, regardless of whether the one analyzing the discourse admits it or not. But discourse analysis does not coincide with hermeneutics, because it formulates a question that hermeneutics can grasp only from the standpoint of reception. And it does so with the metaphorically imprecise concepts of the horizon and the dissolving of that horizon; namely, concepts in accordance with the rules that discursive practices follow.

To be sure, the Foucauldian "discourse about discourse" (*AS*, 267; *AK*, 205) cannot identify the place from which its own speech issues. Foucault's critics have repeatedly reproached him for that. Since discourse analysis cannot think of a speech or action outside of discourse, its own will to knowledge remains repressive for Manfred Frank; that is, it is only traceable to a will to power.[7] Jürgen Habermas argues in a similar fashion when he maintains that in respect to his own genealogical historical writing, Foucault does not think "genealogically"[8] and that tracing the will to knowledge to the will to power can at best only tactically justify Foucault's own discourse. Now Foucault himself draws attention to this dilemma in the ironically entitled "Conclusion" of *The Archaeology of Knowledge*. He has his fictional partner question the legitimacy of the discourse: "What then is the title of your discourse, where does it come from, and from where does it derive its right to speak? How is it legitimated?" (*AS*, 267; *AK*, 205). Either, so argues the fictional critic, Foucault interprets his own discourse as mere description, in which case it lapses into the naïveté of positivism, or he understands it as "interrogation radicale" (i.e., the placing into question of Western philosophy), in which case he must identify the discourse as philosophical. First of all, Foucault responds helplessly ("I admit that this question embarrasses me") but then offers a clue to his own understanding of himself, which is truly nothing that could satisfy the critic:

> *Mon discours, loin de déterminer le lieu d'où il parle, esquive le sol où il pourrait prendre appui.* (*AS,* 267)
>
> My discourse, far from determining the locus in which it speaks, is avoiding the ground on which it could find support. (*AK,* 205)

The discourse that investigates the real historical ground of other discourses seeks to avoid what it could make out to be its own ground. Not only is Foucault unable to name the place from where he speaks, but he also develops a principle out of the groundlessness of his discourse. If it is assumed in these sentences that Foucault in fact describes what he does, then the question arises as to how texts look that emphasize in this manner their own groundlessness. Stated otherwise, how do the discursive conditions at the margins, to which his own texts are subject, shape these texts, and what processes are used in order to render them powerless? Thus, a discourse analysis of Foucault's texts? More likely, an attempt to inform hermeneutics with the interrogatory directive of discourse analysis. Therefore, heterodoxy in respect to Foucault as well.

On the Difficulty of the Beginning

"None may enter into discourse on a specific subject unless he has satisfied certain conditions or if he is not, from the outset, qualified to do so" ("OD," 225).

In December 1970, Foucault held his inaugural lecture at the Collège de France. With his appointment to this institute, rich with tradition (in the nineteenth century, Michelet and Renan, among others, taught there), he had achieved what an academic can achieve in France: a research professorship that freed him from teaching and examination duties and a recognition of his works that exceeded the bounds of his discipline. The inaugural lecture, particularly when it occurs at an establishment with as much scientific authority as the Collège de France, is an extremely ritualized genre of speech. The admission of the newly chosen colleague is carried out by the teaching staff of the college. By their (silent) presence, the assembled scientists lend authority to the speech of the new colleague.

How does the discourse analyst Foucault, who had made the forces that weigh upon discourse a theme of his work, act in a situation in which he himself as the speaker is subject to the requirements of a genre intended to confer legitimacy upon the speaker? He can neither pass over in silence the forces that weigh upon his speech (that would mean to deny his research during a ceremony to recognize it), nor can he break his speech up in dadaistic fashion by throwing into question the institution (that would come down to declining the position). He is thus faced with two impossible options. A conceivable solution would have been to thematize the institutional forces that underlie the genre of an inaugural lecture. In a reflective manner, he would thus have related his own approach to research to a concrete situation. A decade later, Pierre Bourdieu would sketch such a "lecture to the inaugural lecture" at the beginning of his inaugural lecture to the Collège de France—an elegant solution of the problem that fulfills institutional demands (the one giving the talk literally holds a lecture) and that ironically undoes this fulfillment (the thematization of the inaugural lecture as a genre reveals its ritualistic character). Moreover, Bourdieu did not hold an inaugural lecture about inaugural lectures but was content to signal its possibility.[9]

More radically than Bourdieu, Foucault broke at the outset of his lecture with the conventions of the genre, according to which the speaker is obligated not only to present his previous scientific work and a program for future research but also to present himself as a researcher justifiably called to the Collège de France. While it is expected that the lecturer will make himself visible during his talk, Foucault admits that he would like to dismiss that expectation.

> *Dans le discours qu'aujourd'hui je dois tenir, et dans ceux qu'il me faudra tenir ici, pendant des années peut-être, j'aurais voulu pouvoir me glisser subrepticement. Plutôt que de prendre la parole, j'aurais voulu être enveloppé par elle, et porté bien au-delà de tout commencement possible. J'aurais aimé m'apercevoir qu'au moment de parler une voix sans nom me précédait depuis longtemps: il m'aurait suffi alors d'enchaîner, de poursuivre la phrase, de me loger, sans qu'on y prenne bien garde, dans ses interstices, comme si elle m'avait fait signe en se tenant, un instant, en suspens. De commencement, il*

n'y en aurait donc pas; et au lieu d'être celui dont vient le discours, je serais plutôt au hasard de son déroulement, une mince lacune, le point de sa disparition possible. (*OD*, 7f)

> I would really like to have slipped imperceptibly into this lecture, as into all the others I shall be delivering, perhaps over the years ahead. I would have preferred to be enveloped in words, borne way beyond all possible beginnings. At the moment of speaking, I would like to have perceived a nameless voice, long preceding me, leaving me merely to enmesh myself in it, taking up its cadence, and to lodge myself, when no one was looking, in its interstices as if it had paused an instant, in suspense, to beckon me. There would have been no beginnings: instead, speech would proceed from me, while I stood in its path—a slender gap—the point of its possible disappearance. ("OD," 215)

If one relates the desire not to begin but rather to resume a talk to Foucault's aporetic situation, then as always the concealed admission of the impossibility of the situation becomes recognizable. The analyst of intellectual rituals is himself required to perform a ritual. Foucault responds to this brash demand by questioning the institutionally regulated obviousness of the beginning and by interpreting the metaphor, according to which the speaker seizes the word, as an actual act. This cuts two ways: the appropriation of a discourse by a subject but also the insertion of the subject into an order that obligates and ties the subject to the determination of a statement.

As strange as it might sound, the impulse of Foucauldian writing is not self-expression but rather self-dissolution: "Many write, as I apparently also do, so as no longer to have a face. I am no doubt not the only one who writes in order to have no face"; *AS*, 28; *AK*, 17). In the later introduction to the second volume of the *History of Sexuality*, he calls the motive for writing the wish to free himself of himself ("se déprendre de soi-même"; *UP*, 14). The disappearance of the self and its concrete experience into the universality of language transforms writing into a deed that is as aporetic as it is paradoxical. Only in the mode of losing the self does self-experience seem possible. Foucault lends Blanchot's thought an additional twist by relating it to the discourse on the regulation of institutions. The self thus experiences that institutions provide it with some relief. In the inaugural lecture, the institution responds to the wish to make oneself unknown through escaping the compulsory beginning as follows: There is absolutely no beginning. What appears to be a beginning is in truth the enactment of a ritual. One only needs to carry it out. And the speaker obeys. After a short pause, marked in the text by an asterisk, he continues, metamorphosed into what the institution has made of him: "Here is the hypothesis I would like to advance this evening [. . .]" ("OD," 216). The irritation that the beginning of the lecture might have aroused among its listeners has disappeared. Everything has an order. The lecturer presents a hypothesis, introduces distinctions, bestows an order.

At the end of the lecture, a certain discomfort may have set in, at least among attentive listeners. To be sure, the speaker obeys the rules, but he obeys them almost too completely. If he has accomplished something, he thanks his teachers exclusively for that. That might simply pass as a topos of modesty. But Foucault continues interpreting his appointment to the Collège de France as honoring his teacher Hyppolite. But there is more. In the last paragraph of the speech, he incorporates that irritating beginning into the ritual. The voice that he would resume is none other than Hyppolite's. The placing into question of the institution is not sublated but rather soaked up, absorbed. By interpreting the start of his lecture in the sense of the institution, he subjects himself to the institution. He is thus not simply performing a ritual, but rather directing a movement of consciousness that lends an appearance of substance to a ritual long emptied of any substance. The illustrious listeners can feel elevated since they are in fact what the institution has made of them: the intellectual elite of the nation. The completed inaugural address is not one that perfectly fulfills the genre but rather one that invites resistance to the believability of the ritual. Truly, the performance walks a fine line that separates it from parody. Additionally, has not the speaker realized the curious desire for self-dissolution, which the beginning of the lecture was about, by submitting himself to the ritual? Foucault fulfills the institutional requirement of self-installation, but he does so by disappearing.

Let us return, however, to the beginning of the inaugural lecture, where the speaker confesses his aversion to the institutionally established beginning of a talk. What is with this hesitation? The stipulations of discourse, which Foucault later presumes, require clarification. In that instance, the discussion is about power and the dangers of discourse ("les pouvoirs et les dangers") as well as of its redoubtable materiality ("redoutable materalité"; *OD,* 11). Dangers for whom? one will ask. For the speaker, whom discourse establishes as the subject of the speech. The beginning is irretrievable. What is apparently the most obvious distinction already contains *in nuce* everything that follows (that can be learned from Derrida's Husserl studies). But of what does the materiality consist that Foucault assigns to discourse? Not in the physical bearer of discourse, in the voice or in the sign of writing. With such language, Foucault seems more likely to claim emphatically to have discovered a new object: *discours,* which is neither the expression of a subject nor the appeal to another subject, nor the designation of some facts. Its materiality exists in nothing other than cutting off the references, which for a traditional understanding of language are constitutive, and thereby reaching "behind" the relations of *discours. Discours* is thus the endless chatter in which human action is enmeshed, the text whose mass, variety, and unforseeability represent that unspecified threat that Foucault talks about.

The attempt to define Foucault's concept of discourse requires a correction. The concept describes not only linguistic utterances in their greatest possible universality but also the individual utterance (like, for example, the inaugural lecture Foucault is about to deliver) and finally, a use of language that is subject to particular rules. Foucault had already called attention to the ambiguity of his concept of discourse in the *Archaeology of Knowledge* and ultimately restricted it to the third meaning.[10] But in *The Order of Discourse* he does not stand by this definition. One might thus conclude that an ambiguous use of a critical concept is essential to his thinking. What speaks for that is the fact that in Foucault's texts, two different interpretations of discourse conflict with each other. The first understands discourse as a form of diffuse chatter whose incalculability poses an enduring danger (but one that is fascinating for Foucault) for human efforts of organization (perhaps one should see an echo of Heidegger's "Man" here). According to the second interpretation, discourse itself is conceived of as a controlled and regulated linguistic praxis, whereby the control mechanisms render the speaker productive (Foucault might well be taking up a thought of Valéry, who insisted not only in his poetics upon the productivity of controls). Therefore, *discours* is simultaneously that which is threatening, that which smashes all order and is a rule-guided order, and also that which is an indifference point of absolute opposites. As we have seen, Foucault designed his inaugural lecture at the Collège de France as one such *discours.* The revolt against and the submission to the institution merge as a single gesture, which is neither one gesture nor the other but rather both gestures in a reflective manner.

Bringing the Mute Ground to Speak

Foucault's critics have repeatedly accused him of being able to identify neither the site nor the possibility of his speaking. Foucault knows that, and by articulating this knowledge, he forces his critics into the unfortunate position of merely repeating what the author says. He disempowers critique by already formulating its argument. One can perhaps go even further. The *discours* on *discours* is incapable of any transcendental grounding since each such attempt repeatedly runs into *discours*.

The question surrounding the status of Foucault's texts is thus certainly not answered. How can texts be determined that neither point to an authorial intention laid out in advance nor seek to be understood in terms of pure description? My answer is: as gesture. The young Lukács developed such a concept in his essay on Kierkegaard. Pushing itself away from the chaotic flow of life and the equivocity of possibility, gesture posits a fixed, unshakable reality, renders the equivocity of existence univocal, and imposes a form upon life: "Gesture is just that movement which clearly expresses univocity, form as the sole path of the absolute in life."[11] By breaking off his engagement with Regine Olsen, Kierkegaard makes life univocal; he becomes the eccentric one who writes and Regine, the wife of a former admirer.

The concept, of course, needs to be freed from the cognitive concept of a philosophy of life, which is where it stands with Lukács. How would a concept of gesture look that is not tensed between the metaphysical poles of life and form but that no more likely means a sign-laden activity circumscribed by previously given societal rules? Gesture would then be an absolute linguistic *Tathandlung*[12] that is not established by rules like the everyday gestures of greeting and civility. It should be called absolute, since its preconceptions will not be explained either by the intentions of the doer or by the requirements that condition its activity. Gesture knows neither a theoretical nor a moral justification; otherwise, it would presume to be valid the conditions at the margins that it has just thrown into question.[13] The gesture is positing. Its certainty is not a result of recourse to something that has grounded it, but more likely, it draws its pathos from a refusal of all claims to be grounded. That is where the reserve of the gesture, its obstinacy in the face of the demand for discussion, stems from. To be sure, something can issue from it, but one cannot go behind it. It knows only two dimensions of time: present and future.

The gesture is neither true nor untrue, it is. It is indebted for the evidence that it uses only to itself, and that means also to its linguistic form. Gestural moments are also found in Nietzsche's philosophy (Descartes's self-instantiation in the *Discourse on Method* as well as Kant's discussion of a Copernican turn also belong here), but only in that moment in which the claim for self-grounding is taken up do thought and gesture coincide.

The gesture of Foucault's thought is that of transgression (his early essay on Bataille is entitled "Préface à la transgression"). The *Histoire de la folie* poses the questions: Can what reason excludes be discussed without subjecting it once again to reason? Can reason be rendered powerless as an organ beyond time for seeking the truth by representing the historicity of its boundaries? Can one think in opposition to reason?

The Order of Things interprets the transgressive gesture differently. Here, it is also a matter of thinking the unthinkable: cracks in historical continuity. At the beginning of the foreword, Foucault inserts a text by Borges that places the most heterogeneous categories for the classification of animals next to one another:

> [. . .] animals are divided into (a) belonging to the Emperor, (b) embalmed, (c) tame, (d) suckling pigs, (e) sirens, (f) fabulous, (g) stray dogs, (h) included in the present classification, (i) frenzied, (j) innumerable, (k) drawn with a very fine camel hair brush, (l) et cetera. (*MC*, 7; *OT*, xv)

In the text by Borges, Foucault sees yet another means to outdo the sentence by Lautréamont, which was so often cited by the surrealists: "beautiful as the fortuitous encounter of an umbrella and a sewing machine on an operating table." If placing unrelated things next to one another is bewildering, Borges also removes from them any shared ground, the mute ground: "[H]e does away with the *site*, the mute ground upon which entities can be juxtaposed" (*MC*, 9; *OT*, xvii). In a precise sense, Borges's text does not present a juxtaposition of things, but rather of orders, which, however, do not offer any indication of their relationship to each other. What Foucault's book presents is a juxtaposition or a succession of orders that have enabled theories and knowledges since the Renaissance. This is what he designates as episteme. By rendering recognizable the bridge between the preclassical, classical, and modern epistemes, he pulls the shared ground out from under Western thought, a ground by which its unity might be thought:

> *En essayant de remettre au jour cette profonde dénivellation de la culture occidentale, c'est à notre sol silencieux et naïvement immobile que nous rendons ses ruptures, son instabilité, ses failles; et s'est lui qui s'inquiète à nouveau sous nos pas.* (*MC*, 16)

> In attempting to uncover the deepest strata of Western culture, I am restoring to our silent and apparently immobile soil its rifts, its instability, its flaws; and it is the same ground that is once more stirring under our feet. (*OT*, xxiv)

The metaphorical talk of the mute or silent ground allows the direction of Foucault's project to be recognized and, moreover, to bring anew the ground to speak. In contrast to the philosophy of Descartes, it is not a matter of securing the stability of the ground but rather of putting that solidity into question. Such thinking can no longer identify the site of its own speaking; it can only point to the fissures that run through Western thought.

The Archaeology of Knowledge makes explicit the impossibility of naming the site of its own speaking. It has been described as Foucault's *Discourse on Method.* That is clearly accurate only if one adds that it is at the same time its reverse. It is not the erection of a firm foundation for the construction of the sciences, but rather the construction of a science without foundation, even without an object that allows itself to be determined with any certainty. After more than one hundred pages of methodological observation come the following, rather bewildering questions:

> *Mais au fait, de quoi ai-je parlé jusqu'ici? Quel a été l'objet de mon enquête? Et il était dans mon propos de décrire quoi?* (*AS,* 105)

> But what, in fact, have I been speaking about so far? What has been the object of my inquiry? And what did I intend to describe? (*AK,* 79)

More than fifty pages of an equally fascinating and irritating search follow in which Foucault seeks through a variety of negations to secure what he calls *énoncé:* That smallest unity of discourse, which is neither a word nor a sentence nor a speech and which ultimately, by dint of the effort dedicated to it, arrives at a minimum of consistency. The rigor of the argument joins with its opposite in such a manner that it includes the observable potential for uncertainty. If there is a surrealist philosophy, not one derived from the texts of the surrealists but rather one that carries out as philosophy the surrealist project to unsecure all schematic thinking, it is most likely to be found with Foucault. Rehabilitation of madness as a manner of thinking, demonstration of the fissures in the assumptions of Western thinking, the outline of a science that is defined at the same time as a labyrinth in which the author can lose himself[14]—these are surrealist gestures of transgressing boundaries.

The gesture, we might say, refuses explanation. As a self-grounding act, it has an absolute understanding of itself. The self's absoluteness is the result of a positing, and that means that it is the opposite of what it intended to be, namely, something dependent on conditions.[15] It does not occur in an empty space. Transgressing boundaries is not without a boundary. And Foucault's philosophical gesture rests on conditions that can be legitimately questioned. By that, I mean less the philosophical tradition in which Foucault is situated and which is denoted by names such as Nietzsche, Bataille, and Blanchot, than I do the constellation of French thinkers of the 1950s that leaves its impression on Foucault. All possible positions of epochal thinking seem to be occupied: Sartre, despite being outside the university, brings together the cultural power of academically recognized philosophers and the prestige of protest thinking; Lévi-Strauss occupies the position of one founding a new science, structural anthropology; Barthes, finally, embodies the type of critic open to everything that simultaneously appears with Brecht and Robbe-Grillet. Foucault experiences the entire epoch as Alexandrian, "the age of commentary to which we belong" ("PT," 760). The question that he must have seen posed before him was most likely: Can a new thought be won from the epoch of commentary?

If the intuition that defines the epoch as Alexandrian is correct, any attempt to think it must be involved in this situation; that is, writing commentary that is not commentary as such. Foucault must invalidate commentary as a textual genre and, at the same time, grant the subjectless speech of commentary the status of a philosophical text. He must turn the limit of rational thinking and what is excluded from it into an object of his thinking without lapsing into the whisper of a pseudopoetic use of speech ("to think the limit; to think the unthinkable; to think language"). He must entrust himself to language in the hope that thought will form itself in language and not hand himself over to the rigor of a rational schooling of thought. Once all paths have been pursued, the construction of a labyrinth becomes an image of possible freedom. When security nets are tensed, the loosening of the pegs to which they are secured seems to be the only meaningful action. In the age of commentary, the only gesture that remains to the philosopher is one that undermines philosophy.

Should one who has sought to subject himself to such thinking call it in the end self-deception? Must it be said that a will to be a subject, a will tensed to the point of breaking apart, forms the basis for the critique of the subject? Must it be said that the longing for self-dissolution is only a need for expression that is interpreted negatively? And that the critique of commentary produces uninterrupted self-commentary? The Foucauldian gesture of thinking does not sublate oppositions but rather crushes them in *discours*.

7. The Truth of Doctor Lacan

A Letter

Bremen, 31 December 1989

Dear Sigi:

Since I begin this letter in the last hours of the old year without prospect of finishing it in this year, the matter must be pressing. Insofar as you have continually urged me to think about Lacan, the matter is in fact pressing, which doesn't exclude the fact that I intend to proceed thoughtfully.

When you faced the demon—and according to my perception of time, it is not that long ago—of what to study, I advised you to choose a field that interested you: philosophy. You had good reasons for the choice, and I as well for my advice. I do not see it any differently today. What concerns me is the question whether you have met the necessary resistance from your teachers, who are certainly good ones but perhaps not for you. (Excuse the tone, which does not correspond to the manner in which we speak to each other.) This letter should confront you with such resistance.

What I criticize in your thinking, I have often told you in conversation and thus do not need to present it again. You devour the philosophical texts of the present, combining them in an endless signifying chain, which is dizzying to the uninformed listener. You also know my advice to remedy your philosophical voracity: precise readings of a difficult text from the philosophical tradition. If, until now, you have not heeded my advice, that is presumably due less to the skepticism of your teachers vis-à-vis interpretation and more to the fact that you are not concerned with the understanding of a text, even if it is a particularly meaningful one, but rather with truth. "There's the rub," as Hamlet says. At the end of your theoretical outline, which moves from Heidegger and/or Adorno through Guattari/Deleuze and culminates in Lacan (I simplify to a fault), you pose implicitly or explicitly the question of truth. Could it be that man as a being marked by a lack necessarily develops a narcissistic ego that is initially secured by a fictive mirror image? And that, as a result, the experience of the unity of the self is bound to a deception whose ground is inaccessible, thus rendering impossible any attempt to undermine it? Would that not constitute an anthropological foundation of Heideggerian ontology? I remain indebted to you for answers to questions of this sort, and I will not relate them belatedly as a letter. I would like, however, to formulate a few questions about your question.

There is nothing objectionable about your asking about the truth, only the manner in which you do. You ask in fact—is it true? Don't we then have to make fundamental anthropological assumptions that are universally valid and transcend historical differences? I can make it easy for myself and bring your Master Lacan into the picture:

> *La perception visuelle d'un homme formé dans un complexe culture tout à fait différent du nôtre, est une perception tout à fait différente de la nôtre.*[1]
>
> The visual perception of a man who has been formed in a completely different visual cultural complex is a completely different visual perception from ours.

And what is valid for perception should also hold for the perception of one's own image in the mirror.

I will not, however, make it too easy for myself, but rather pose your question. That, I think, is how philosophy begins. You ask about truth as one would seek to confirm the factual accuracy of a report. There is a text in which certain assertions of fact are made. One seeks then to discover whether such assertions correspond to something in reality, whether they are correct. The notion of truth that you employ in this matter has a tradition, it asserts truth as the agreement of thought with the thing (*adaequatio rei et intellectus*). Should one not test whether this is Lacan's notion of truth before applying it to his texts? (You see, even the philosopher cannot avoid interpreting except at the cost of a certain naïveté that he presumes to have left behind.)

Outside, the rocket explosions are becoming louder, which, so it seems, are necessary for us to usher in the new year. So I take leave of you for this year, which has given us intellectuals quite a bit to think about.

1 January 1990

To begin the new year with considerations of the notions of truth in Lacan is only to be justified if the investigation, at the very least, opens up the prospect of producing something that is not only of historical philosophical interest. Stated otherwise, when the investigation succeeds in orienting itself to our current historical situation. I am naturally aware that I cannot satisfy the demand that is thereby formulated. That would mean no less than to have penetrated Benjamin's enigmatic dictum about the temporal kernel of truth to the extent that it offers itself as the key to our own current situation. I turn then first to Lacan's notion of truth, knowing full well that by doing so I am performing the typical move of the intellectual who, "first of all," strives to solve the fundamental problem before arriving at reality. But perhaps this is precisely the right move, because it links up with the one competency we intellectuals share. Perhaps we *must* embarrass ourselves when we mean to intervene "in reality." Let me start once more where my first letter ended. When you submit Lacan's theses to the question of truth, you employ a notion of truth inconsistent with the Lacanian one. You seek something outside of linguistic utterance; we might call them facts. That is, according to Lacan, precisely what is not possible. That is initially rather difficult to see, but it becomes understandable when one clarifies that Lacan's notion of truth is read from the psychoanalytic conversation (more precisely, on a particular interpretation of that situation). The psychoanalyst is first of all nothing other than a "talking cure," just as Breuer's first patient called it. The speech of the patient is the one thing that the patient and the analyst can hold onto. In it, the patient develops a fragmentary picture of his past. Now Lacan emphasizes that it is not a matter of whether the patient actually experienced or only imagined what is reported. Far more decisive is that he accepts as his history the history that he tells the analyst.

> *C'est bien cette assomption par le sujet de son histoire, en tant qu'elle est constituée par la parole adressée à l'autre, qui fait le fond de la nouvelle méthode à quoi Freud donne le nom de psychanalyse.* (*Ecrits,* 257)

It is good this assumption by the subject of his history insomuch as that history is constituted by the word addressed to the other, which forms the foundation of the new method to which Freud gave the name psychoanalysis.

The activity of the psychoanalyst is strictly confined to listening to the patient and confirming to him at the end that he is none other than the one depicted in conversations. Even empty speech, chatter, in which, according to Mallarmé, the word is transmitted like a worn coin, is evidence for Lacan that the word constitutes truth ("que la parole constitue la vérité"; *Ecrits,* 252). Solely the word spoken here and now attests to the truth of the event and grounds truth in the present of speaking, which is a speaking to another.

This notion of truth deviates most radically from that of the philosophical tradition by joining truth to the here and now of a present situation from which the past is fixed just as the future is sketched. Truth is constructed not between utterances and facts that can be verified outside of language; it is constructed solely within language. Its place is not eternity, not even the past, but solely the present. Truth is not related to facts but emerges instead to the effect of speech in an asymmetrical system of communication.

You will object that it is not a matter of Lacan's notion of truth but rather of something else, namely, whether or not its central theorems (the mirror stage, primary narcissism, etc.) can and must be grasped as a fundamental ontology in accordance with Heidegger and whether that might not force us to seize upon alienation much more "deeply" than what has occurred, for example, in the Marxist tradition. In short, it is a matter for you of the facts of these assumptions, regardless of whether one designates them as "truth."

Well roared, Lion! Or so I permit myself to recall in line with Lacan: roared means to say "spoken." If I understand you correctly, you interpret the construction of the mirror phase—Lacan himself once called it "ma construction"—as a quasi-fundamental ontological assumption upon which basis human fate is explained. That is certainly a possible mode of reading, but it is, if I may say so, un-Lacanian. For Lacan there is, strictly speaking, no extralinguistic phenomenon that one could talk about. Whatever we talk about is always already an interpreted phenomenon; the *factum brutum* is an illusory construction.

> *Les événements s'engendrent dans une historisation primaire, autrement dit l'histoire se fait déjà sur la scène où on la jouera une fois écrite, au for interne comme au for extérieur.* (*Ecrits,* 261)

> The events engender themselves in a primary historicization, stated otherwise: history makes itself on the scene where one will play it, once written, in the interior as in the exterior.

In *Discours de Rome,* Lacan explained it by using a historical example: An uprising in Faubourg Saint Antoine was experienced by participants in the seventeenth century as victory or defeat of the Frond Parliament or the absolutist court and in the nineteenth century as the victory or defeat of the proleteriat or the bourgeoisie. The memory trace that these events leave behind depends on this "primary historicization."

I will not go into the far-reaching consequences that this thesis could have for historical description, but rather return to our question. If one pursues the interpretation of the theorem of the mirror stage that I have ascribed to you, then Lacan is embroiled in a performative self-contradiction (as Habermas calls it). On the one hand, he maintains that extralinguistic facts are not accessible; on the other, he introduces such a fact with its quasi-ontological assumption about the construction of the self. This interpretation is in no way compelling. It is, to be precise, possible to read the theorem of the mirror stage otherwise—as narrative, in fact. Read as such within Lacanian theory, it can very well lay a claim to truth. All that is required is that the respective listener confirm his story to the narrator Lacan. Herein may lie the function of analysis for the analyst. If the patient, at the end of analysis, sees through his phantasm as phantasm and recognizes his ego as a fictive, narcissistically posited mirroring, he confirms to the analyst the truth of that narrative, which has served the patient as a schema in order to relate his own history.

I sense that what has been said doesn't convince you. Is the theorem of the mirror stage correct or not? There is nothing left for me to do—but to speak further. What does the narrative report? Of the small child's original experience, of the fragmentation of its body ("le corps morcelé"), of the jubilant experience of completeness that he initially experiences but not in relation to his own body but rather to the image in the mirror and thereafter to the bodies of children of like age, and finally, of the narcissistic positing of this mirroring. The original (mirroring) self is therefore fictional and estranged simultaneously: an aggressivity, directed outwardly as well as against its own self, would come from this self, based on its narcissistic role. The self can free itself from the imaginary illusion of its ego through entering the symbolic order; this occurs through estrangement of a different sort. If the entry into the symbolic is not completely successful, and it almost never is, the adult continues to live in the delusionary world of the infantile imagination, from which only analysis can free him.

I'm not concerned with a reconstruction of Lacan's theory, but rather in making the structure of the narrative recognizable, the truth (fact) of which you asked about so persistently. That it is a matter of a myth of origination will not have escaped you, one that is entirely comparable to the story of original sin and the redemption of mankind by the Son of God. And tales cannot be authenticated through references to facts. The fact that the small infant visibly takes pleasure in its own mirror image no more confirms the truth of Lacan's narrative than does the proof that in a Near-Eastern province of the Roman Empire a man was crucified who was called the King of the Jews confirm the truth of Christian doctrine. In both cases, this is possible only because it is actually believed, that is, taken for granted. With that, I have answered both my question and yours at the same time—and completely in a Lacanian sense. If Lacan's narrative helps you come to better terms with your "self," then it is your truth. You "know" your self to be a mere mirroring narcissistically cast, just as the adherents of Schopenhauer "know" that individuation is in the end only deception. And just as insight in Lacanian theory allows you to recognize the narcissistic delusion and to restrict, if not break, its effective powerful hold, so too for its adherents does Schopenhauerian philosophy rip away the veil of Maya, delusional individuation, and enable them to be freed through this recognition from the constraints to which they are subject as individuals (above all, fear of death). Philosophy is practically renewed by Schopenhauer and thereby responds to the persistence of a metaphysical need in modernity. In its own way, Lacan's philosophy does the same. To be sure, it has an overtly diabolical element, which becomes ever more apparent in its notion of truth. This is also where my attempt to argue against Lacan would begin. In any case, a hopeless attempt, since his theory dismisses discussion. Has it not struck you that Lacan rarely refutes other schools of psychoanalytic thought with arguments but instead shrugs them off contemptuously? I recognize that as more than a polemical mode of representation, namely, as the necessary form of a theory that ultimately grounds truth in the act of its pronouncement. If one accepts the thesis of "primary historicization," if one admits that there is nothing outside of interpretation with which to connect this historicization for purposes of measurement, then true is what participants in an asymmetrical communication system represent as true. For the National Socialists, it was true that the Jews were "an inferior race" that threatened the "Germanic race." With Lacan, it would be argued that there might be other "truths" but no possible site from which the National Socialists could be disproved.

I hear your objection. But in the *Prosa der Moderne* you yourself referred to Lacan's notion of truth according to which truth is constructed between subjects. Right! Certainly, one cannot infer from its plausibility for the understanding that plays out between analyst and patient the notion's validity in other fields; that would constitute an overreaching of the concept. I have also tried to think it through with Hegel's *Phenomenology of Spirit,* in which the work is introduced as the third moment of reference between author and recipient in order to understand the construction of what Hegel called "the thing itself" (*die Sache selbst*)[2] and what can perhaps be translated with the truth content of the work. The difference between the two positions consists in the fact that Hegel, in contrast to Lacan, knows an outside. He calls it "doing" (*Tun*).

Certainly, for Lacan, there is also an outside to the delusion of the imagination and the estrangement due to the symbolic order; he designates it in the *Discours de Rome* with a phrase taken from Heidegger, *Sein-zum-Tode,* "being unto death" ("la réalisation subjective de l'être-pour-la-mort"; *Ecrits,* 279; "the subjective realization of being unto death"). In curious fashion, Lacan projects the Heideggerian "being unto death" into the constellation of the Hegelian battle for prestige, thereby changing the meaning of the latter. What interests him is not the crossing over of work and power or the dialectic of recognition (in any case, not in this instance) but rather different formations of preparedness for death, the highest of which appears in suicide, "that desperate affirmation of life."

> *La liberté de l'homme s'inscrit toute dans le triangle constituant de la renonciation qu'il impose au désir de l'autre par la menace de la mort pour la jouissance de fruits de son servage,—du sacrifice consenti de sa vie pour les raisons qui donnent à la vie humaine sa mesure,—et du renoncement suicide du vaincu frustrant de sa victoire le maître qu'il abandonne à son inhumaine solitude.* (*Ecrits,* 320)

> Man's freedom is entirely inscribed within the constituting triangle of the renunciation that he imposes on the desire of the other by the menace of death for the enjoyment of the fruits of his serfdom—of the consented—to sacrifice of his life for the reasons that give to human life its measure—and of the suicidal renunciation of the vanquished partner, depriving of his victory the master whom he abandons to inhuman solitude. (*Eng.,* 204)

Although Lacan speaks of the suicide of the vanquished, he hits upon a mien of which only the master is capable within the Hegelian model that he assesses (then the slave is determined precisely by the fact that he gives in to his fear of death). According to Lacan, freedom is possible only for the lonesome subject in the face of death and not for human society. It is the freedom of the master who knows only one act—dying.

Light falls from here on the theory of primary historicization. The Hegelian master, whom Lacan thinks through in Heideggerian terms, does nothing. This is a matter for the slave who works on objects for the master. The master knows nothing of the resistance of things; he lives entirely in language in which reality constantly inverts itself for him. The only resistance he meets is his own death. Lacan has death in mind as that which is opposed to the master and that guarantees the truth of his speech. His speech grants the listeners the simple option of submitting to speech or of excluding themselves from participation in truth. *Tertium non datur.* For the one speaking, the following holds: He does not offer a philosophical opinion, with which others can contest the recognition of truth, but rather embodies his theory. It is founded on the inaccessible experience of absolute preparedness for death and is therefore not refutable as well.

Allow me in concluding to slip into the role of the master so as, in any case, to apply Lacan to Lacan, which I certainly fear Lacanians will appreciate as little as once orthodox Marxists did the attempts of their unorthodox friends to apply Marx to Marx.

For each of Lacan's readers and listeners, it is something quite familiar that in neither his texts nor his lectures does Lacan restrict himself to presenting correlations and developing arguments. It is far more a matter of the text as text. One can see in that a literary bonus and either tolerate it as something that inhibits understanding or enjoy it as something that is aesthetically charming. In both instances, however, the reader seeks the essential not in the text but rather behind it in that which constitutes its content: in the reconstructable theorem of the mirror stage, the structure of desire, and the linguistic character of the unconscious.

What certainly follows from such a reading of Lacan's texts, which, if I don't deceive myself, is also yours, is its obliviousness to Lacan's understanding of language, which always emphasizes that the speech of the patient, even if it is only empty speech, is to be taken seriously as the site where truth can reveal itself. It might well be that the truth of the Lacanian text is not to be found where you look for it—in a meaning of the text that you construct—but rather *ailleurs,* in another place. In short, I ask myself whether it isn't possible to read Lacan's texts as he reads a patient's monologue.

Now, you will presumably reply that Lacan's texts, in contrast to the patient's monologue, are not empty speech but rather claim to be *full speech,* at least according to the intention of the author. One could respond to that as follows: If Lacan takes his theory of language seriously, then he cannot make an exception for his own linguistic utterances. Language, according to the theory, is not directed at a sharing of information but rather at an unveiling of the truth in speech. The truth that I thereby track would be one that the texts "says," which does not mean that Lacan must also say it. On the contrary, Lacan's theory of the self speaks for the fact that Lacan is not the one speaking in his texts; rather, it is the other.

As I write, I sense your resistance to what has been said. You must, however, realize that it is resistance to Lacan's theory.

I begin with a comment. Lacan takes extraordinary care to localize his texts in an extraordinary manner, whether he already offers in the text itself details about the time and the place of the lecture and its first listeners or whether he adds these details later in the form of a forward or prefatory remarks. Certainly, one should not assume that this is merely scientific pedantry, particularly since in the same texts Lacan often fails to denote any more clearly the addressees of his polemic. So what is the issue, then? The connection with his theory of truth is striking. It is one that always connects truth to a specific object, but the connection does not explain the phenomenon.

I suspect a deep, affective relationship to his own speech that wholly connects the ego's feelings of self-worth to the act of speaking. The manner in which Lacan introduces the mirror stage in his lectures suggests as much. He does not simply present the centerpiece of his theory, but rather he calls it to mind. One is tempted to say that he introduces it in the form of an anecdote—a curious form when one considers that it is his declared aim to make psychoanalysis a science. In *Propos sur la causalité* of 1946 and *Le Stade du miroir* of 1949, he reports that already in 1936 at the International Congress for Psychoanalysis in Marienbad, he had presented the theory ("ma construction," "mon stade du miroir"; *Ecrits,* 184, 186). Now, this could not be a matter of anything else but an attempt to reclaim for himself the discovery of a theory (what also speaks in favor of that is the reference to a 1939 book of a certain Lhermitte, which Lacan introduces with the following remark: "L'Idée a fait son chemin"; *Ecrits,* 185; "The idea makes its way").

Since, as Freud has shown, psychological facts can rarely be traced to a single cause, should we not be satisfied with this condition? In the aforementioned 1946 text, we in fact come across a clue that serves to shed light on his fascination with the word. During a lecture on the mirror stage at the Congress in 1936 he was interrupted by Ernest Jones, the chairperson of the London Psychoanalytic Society, after only ten minutes. Apparently, the young scientist, who was speaking for the first time before an international forum of his colleagues, found the event traumatic. A full twenty-three years later, in a 1959 lecture dedicated to the memory of Ernest Jones, he referred to the event as well as to his reaction of 1946:

> *[L]'impériosité sans ménagement pour le nouveau que nous étions à Marienbad, [. . .] rapport épidermique dont la pique s'avoue encore après la guerre en l'un de nos écrits.* (*Ecrits,* 697)
>
> The imperiosity without consideration for the newcomer who we were at Marienbad, [. . .] epidermal relation of which the prick avows itself again after the war in one of our own works.

In 1946, Lacan had permitted himself a few friendly remarks about Jones's character and so ironically introduced Jones's qualification to be chair of the psychoanalytic society.

It seems reasonable to trace Lacan's silence after this event (he published only an encyclopedia article during that time) not, as he does, as a result of the political situation but rather as an indication of how deeply wounded he was by the revocation of the word by one of the recognized spokespersons of psychoanalysis. The theory that he wanted to talk about but was unable to bring to speech he abandoned; instead, he worked it out further and, with reference to the definition of delusion in Hegel's *Phenomenology of Spirit,* radicalized it as a theory of the paranoid knowledge of the infant (*Ecrits,* 171ff, 180).

Lacan does not deny the painful wound but rather refers to it (*Repères bibliographique* lists rather pedantically the exact time and place of the Marienbad lecture: 3 August at 15:40; *Ecrits,* 917). He thereby reevaluates the event and transforms the traumatic failure into the originary moment of a correct theory. Inasmuch as it arises from defeat, this becomes its seal. How can a theory's lack of recognition ground its truth? It can do so only if the subject succeeds in repeating the scene and reversing its signs. For him it is not a matter of how convincing the theory is but rather of reconstructing the scene during its rehearsal. Therefore, Lacan recalls his 1936 lecture.

Apparently, he has not only talked around the original scene of 1936, but he has also adjusted it or resituated it at a later time. At the beginning of the so-called *Discourse du Rome* and again at the beginning of the 164 Seminar XX, it is a question of events that show a marked parallel to that of 1936. In opposition to the "excommunication" by the International Society for Psychoanalysis, which had questioned the legitimacy of his teaching, he brings Braudel, Lévi-Strauss, and the psychoanalyst Henry Ey into the fray, the last of which authenticated the truth of his teachings by their participation in the first meeting of the seminar in the "Ecole des Haute Etude." Once again, reference to a—contested—article is not lacking about whose themes he says "made present by the fact that I am here in the posture that is mine to introduce always the same questions—*what* is psychoanalysis?" ("présentifiées par le fait que je suis ici, dans la posture qui est la mienne, pour introduire toujours cette même question—qu'est-ce que la psychanalyste?") The original scene must always be repeated.

"But what does that have to do with Lacan's theory?" you might ask and thereby anticipate my answer. I will summarize quickly, since this letter should not become too long for you. The theory of primary historicization as well as that of speech as the site of truth can be interpreted as theoretical fantasizing about the experience at Marienbad, for the dialectical operation of reevaluation that Lacan performs in respect to the trauma of 1936 can only be accomplished without remainder, if there is no *factum brutum,* if truth is constituted solely within the realm of language without relationship to an extralinguistic reality.

In the fairy tale of the dumb Peter, who is ignored at home, leaves, and marries the king's daughter, the hero returns voluntarily in the end to the place of suffering so as to enjoy the triumph when the people learn that he is now king. . . .

8. Derrida

GL

One can read Derrida's *Glas*—provided one can read it all—as an attempt to allow Hegel and surrealism to appear next to each other in a duel of discourses. It should be said that the text does not thematize the relation of surrealism to Hegel, nor is it even about surrealism. Rather, of the two columns printed in parallel fashion in the book, the one would not be possible without the surrealist "invention" of *écriture automatique.* Although in no fashion exclusively so, the text dedicated to Genet, which is simultaneously a text about Derrida's own writing, reads as a form of automatic interpretation. The author allows himself to be led by sound associations, plays with the language and the dictionary (above all that of Littré), and picks up on digressions that, perhaps coincidentally, present themselves. Opposite that, on the left side of the text is a Hegel exegesis that pursues the question: What is sublation? There is first of all no exchange between the two blocks of texts; they appear more likely to repel each other.

> *L'une [des deux colonnes] assure, garde, assimile, intériorise, idéalise, relève la chute dans le monument [. . .]. L'autre—laisse tomber le reste. Risquant de revenir au même.* (*Glas,* 7)[1]
>
> The first [of the two columns] assumes, guards, assimilates, interiorizes, idealizes the fall into the monument [. . .]. The other—lets the remain(s) fall. Running the risk of coming down to the same. (*Eng.,* 1–2)

It might displease Derrida, whose aim it is to move beyond the hierarchical opposition of dissimilar terms without sublating them in syntheses, if one, in fact, rediscovers in the arrangement of his text just what he wanted to avoid: a hierarchical opposition. He will certainly attempt to set this in motion. He hopes that both discourses deconstruct one another simultaneously and thus sound the death knell for the meaning of each.

> *Les glas, tels que nous les aurons entendus, sonnent la fin de la signification, du sens et du signifiant.* (*Glas,* 39)

> The *glas*es [knells], such as we shall have heard them, toll the end of signification, of sense, of the signified. (*Eng.,* 31)

The reader, in any case, who expects to find this program formulated in Derrida's text, is taught something else toward the end of the book: "Je fais ce que je ne dis pas, à peu près, je ne dis jamais ce que je fais" (*Glas,* 254; "I do what I do not say, almost, I never say what I do"; *Eng.,* 227). How should one interpret the many places in which the author talks about his text? Either it is merely a matter of mere phatic textual passages, a murmur, to convince the reader to continue reading; or they are to lead the reader down false roads. If it holds that "I never say what I do," then the sentences in which the author comments on his writing are invalidly made sentences. Certainly, the reverse can hold. The author has commented on this writing and would like at this later date to destroy it. Therefore, he crosses it out but in such a manner that it remains legible. We thus have two texts: the author's comments about his own writing and the destruction of that text. Since no instance in the text can be made out that would resolve this contradiction, it remains. *Glas* or meaning? More likely a game with the reader.

If the author plays a (his) game with us, nothing is left for us to do save play with his texts. The author replies, in effect, to the question, "What is the aim of the game?" with two texts, as follows: "There is a wish to make the writing ungraspable" (*Eng.,* 64); "On veut rendre l'écriture imprenable, bien sûr" (*Glas,* 76). Mastery of the text is ripped away from the reader. He cannot get beyond looking at the other half of the page. Suddenly, the two texts mix and the boundary blurs, a boundary that at first seems to be drawn so sharply by not only the white spaces between columns but also the other thematic and the other procedure:

> *Si j'écris deux textes à la fois, vous ne pourrez pas me châtrer. Si je délinéarise, j'érige. Mais en même temps, je divise mon acte et mon désir. Je—marque*

la division et vous échappant toujours, je simule sans cesse et ne jouis nulle part. Je me châtre moi-même—je me reste ainsi—et je "joue à jouir." Enfin presque. (*Glas*, 77)

If I write two texts at once, you will not be able to castrate me. If I delinearize, I erect. But at the same time I divide my act and my desire. I—mark(s) the division, and always escaping you, I simulate unceasingly and take my pleasure nowhere. I castrate myself—I remain(s) myself thus—and I "play at coming." Finally almost. (*Eng.*, 65)

The master is the great castrator. Everyone is conscripted into his system; one can only repeat after him. It is impossible to break out of the system. This is demonstrated by the text about Hegel. It proceeds with citations and comments in the hope of finding a hole somewhere in which the demolition sentence might be placed, but it is nowhere to be found. The absolute phantasm cannot fail (*Glas*, 251). The monument stands there vertically and threateningly; there is no getting around it. But perhaps it can be shaken by a remark spoken in passing.

The master thinker threatens the small philosopher-author with castration. Can the latter escape the threat? By writing two texts simultaneously, taking the meaning away from his text (castrating himself), which is always one text or aims to be. The solution to the problem is not the ambiguous text, since ambiguity can always be translated into conceptual opposites and sublated, thus remaining inside the Hegelian system. Rather, the solution is the split text, the text that is two but has one author.

Of these two texts, one is always centered around Hegel's fundamental category, sublation ("sublation is being"). Along with Hegel, it finds sublation everywhere at work. The other text, however, is decentered, fragmented.

Les morceaux, que je coupe et couds dans le texte désigné par le dénommé Genet ne doivent ni détruire sa forme ou casser son souffle [. . .], ni en recomposer ou ressaisir l'intégrité dans un de ces filets—formel ou sémantique—que nous avons feint de lancer et de relancer sans compter: seulement pour montrer ou plutôt entraîner au-delà de toute manifestation que le filet n'opère que dans la mesure où il est redevable d'un reste. Il ne retient que des restes, de monumentales dépouilles, et laisse tomber le reste. (*Glas*, 190f)

The morsels, which I cut and sew in the text designated by the one named Genet, must neither destroy its form [n]or quash its (prompting) breath [. . .], nor recompose or recapture its integrity in one of those nets—

formal or semantic—that we have feigned to throw and rethrow without counting: only in order to show or rather to draw beyond any manifestation that the net operates only insofar as it is beholden to a remain(s). It only retains remains, some monumental carcasses, and then lets the remain(s) fall (to the tomb). (*Eng.*, 169)

That no interpretation fully grasps the text it interprets is an insight of hermeneutics that lends the interpretation process the structure of an infinite delay. Derrida apparently means something else. He understands his text on Genet to be a type of interpretive game that should not achieve precisely that which interpretation otherwise is resolved to do: clarification of the text. As such, he must always blur the trace of meaning through a torrent of words wherever the trace threatens to be readable:

> *Et si tout ce labeur de galérien s'était épuisé à émettre (le mot* émettre *me paraît intéressant mais insatisfaisant, il faudrait dire aussi oindre, induire, enjoindre, enduire)*[2]
>
> *GL*
>
> *je ne dis pas le signifiant GL, ni le phonème GL, ni le graphème GL. La marque ce serait mieux si on etendait bien ce mot ou si on lui ouvrait les oreilles; ni même la marque donc [. . .]*
>
> *gl reste gl* (*Glas*, 137)

> And if all this galley-slaving had worn itself out with emitting (the word *emitting* strikes me as interesting but unsatisfying, it would also be necessary to say anointing, inducing, enjoining, smearing)
>
> GL
>
> I do not say either the signifier GL, or the phoneme GL, or the grapheme GL. Mark would be better, if the word were well understood, or if one's ears were open to it; not even mark then [. . .]
>
> gl remain(s) gl (*Eng.*, 119)

Under no circumstances should the reader master Genet's text (*Glas*, 229), and also not Derrida's. As what, then, does a text offer itself once it withdraws indications of meaning by making itself unreadable? Not, as one might perhaps think, as an artwork, but rather as a fetish. And so stands at the end of the Genet text, in a beautifully logical manner, a theory of the fetish as that object about which an unambiguous decision is impossible.

We have read Derrida's texts about Derrida as if they had not been erased but instead were there as an aid that the author had made available to the reader of his book. But if the following sentence holds, "I do what I do not say, almost, I never say what I do" (*Glas,* 254; *Eng.,* 227), then all indexes for reading are to be understood as ambushes that Derrida sets for the reader intent on a univocity of meaning.

Is it true that the writer who denies his text the right to say something castrates himself? He may have an eye out for something definite, but it is in fact a refusal of anything definite, and he achieves that. If anyone is castrated, it is the reader. Derrida, as it were, knocks out of his hands not only the book that he is trying to read but also all books insofar as he understands those books to be sites of meaning. The castration of the other is concealed by talk of self-castration in which the author presents himself as a new Abraham who simulated castration with circumcision and was the more powerful for it. "The Jewish mystery [. . .] is finally discovered as an empty space" (*Eng.,* 50), so Derrida comments on the thoughts of the young Hegel about the spirit of Judaism. Subjection to an empty shrine as the enactment of power—is that not the phantasm that Derrida's text both pronounces and conceals? By sacrificing the (sayable, decidable) meaning of a text, he grants it an unfathomable depth. The sacrifice of meaning is simulation; it endlessly longs for meaning and produces just what it seems to withhold: meaning, which it simultaneously withdraws again and again. The author of the operation, who appears to have abandoned any unity of the function of the author, shows himself to be the author of a particular order.

9. Heidegger

Thinking and Death

Nietzsche's phrase, "God is dead," is a strange thing.[1] At first glance, it seems to be clear and univocal, but the longer we think about it, the more opaque is its meaning. Finally, the suspicion arises that it might not make any sense. As long as we presume to understand it, we have no difficulty transforming the sentence into another of like meaning. "God is dead" says, then, we live in a world without God; that is, we live in the world. But does our sentence, from which God's name has been erased, agree with that of Nietzsche's? Even the linguist's knowledge, which tells us that the sentence is agrammatical since it cannot be said about God as an immortal essence that he is dead, is no more satisfying since it halts any movement of thought before it begins.

Perhaps we can better track the meaning of the sentence if we neither reformulate it nor attempt to circumscribe its absurdity but rather say the sentence aloud to ourselves in its original form. We will thereby make the discovery that the sentence acquires a different ring and a different meaning depending on the placement of the intonation and the caesura: "*God* / is dead." "God *is* / dead." "God is / *dead*." Particularly, the second way of reading the sentence, in which the copula is stressed, deserves attention: "God *is* / dead." That means the same as: "God *is* as the one who is dead." There can be no doubt that he is but the manner in which he is, is as a dead one. Now, we attempt once more to formulate the sentence: God is present to us as one who is absent. Our relationship to him is the lack of a relationship. Stated otherwise, we have forgotten God. The sentence does not say something about the existence or nonexistence of God but rather about our relationship to God, and it establishes the relationship as a lack.

The basic form of Heideggerian thought has been revealed to us through a reading of Nietzsche's sentence.[2] Emphasizing the copula brings the semantic paradox of the sentence to the fore and makes being dead recognizable as a manner in which God exists for us: present as one who is absent. The opposition of two modes of being is thereby stilled; this cessation is not the one of momentary shock, which Benjamin had discussed, but rather one conditioned by circumstance. It does not occur; instead, it has already occurred: a polarity that we cannot get beyond. The dialectic is thereby detained, and at the same time a horizon is opened up for the self into which it enters as if under a spell. Under this spell, all objects are transformed, or more precisely, there are no objects just as there is no longer a subject. Instead, the self moves in an always already determined space that at the same time always seems wholly indeterminate. It has lost all usual grounds of orientation since there are no more oppositions.

What does the self perceive in that space of experience that God's presencing absence opens up for it? Neither itself as subject nor things as possible objects to work on, but rather the abandonment by God of the world. This presents itself as the senseless drive of everyone or as boredom, and combining the two, it presents itself as a speech that coats all doing and letting (*Tun und Lassen*) with meanings of which there is no indicating whether they apply. But the self finds itself again in this world as the indeterminate presentiment of a lack that it is unable to define. How should it designate that lack after God has died? Insofar as the lack is its lack, it holds to itself. But this self, which it would hold onto, is not there at all. It has to create itself.

In this situation, the self turns back to the sentence that led it away from any previous certainty in its thinking and in which it suspects therefore the ground of a new certainty. Once again, it says the sentence to itself and writes it down. In the process it discovers that it can record the sentence in various ways, as such: "God is—death." God is the death. In the place of a relationship to God arrives death, more precisely, my death. The self clings to the certainty of its death and finds anchoring in its finitude. It lives wholly in the future, in its being unto death. The present becomes for it something of the past, and the time that separates it from its corporeal death, indifferent (*gleichgültig*). For the self, it is not time that retains its physiognomy through plans and impediments, but rather duration, whose brevity or length is not crucial; for the self is already dead, just like the heroes of tragedy who are resolved to die.

Everything, however, is completely different. As it did before, the self lives afterward with others in a world abandoned by God, worries about tomorrow, struggles to gain small advantage, and is therefore a part of the hustle and bustle whose meaninglessness it has seen through. However it might otherwise maintain itself, the world remains ever present in the provisionally impossible experience of its own death.

Where, however, does the self in fact live? In the bustle of the world or in that place which death has disclosed to it? The only possible answer is: It necessarily lives in both places. It stands in the everyday, asserts itself there, retreats to here, but is never able to escape the hustle and bustle. And at the same time it is at the other site, that of its own death from where the hustle and bustle can be recognized for what it is. The self therefore lives in two "places" (Heidegger calls them authentic and inauthentic), which, however, are not separated from one another in terms of this world and the hereafter but rather can be experienced in the one world in which we live. This world is "first and foremost" the hustle and bustle in which we are not ourselves and yet retain simultaneously the possibility of grasping ourselves in the impossible experience of our own death. It is absolute equivocity, disaster and salvation in one.

Let us once again make clear the movement of thought that we have followed. Nietzsche's sentence about the death of God exposed the world to the self as one that knows God only as something absent. In this world, the hustle and bustle rules; without respite and direction, it moves everything, and without interruption, it declares and explains itself. Yet, in this confusion of discourses, it cannot be determined which one hits upon the matter that it presumes to consider and which one misses. The one of the everyday, constantly interpreting itself, is equivocal. Everything would thus be a matter of making it univocal. Death—at least for the self—is univocal. It brings everything to end and so determines everything. Here, so it seems, is where univocity is to be won. But death should not be carried out freely; instead, it should illuminate the darkness of human endeavor. It is not a matter of bringing the self out of the world but rather of bringing it to itself in the world. The death that the self grasps is its certain future, whose arrival, however, is undetermined. But the self is incapable of truly grasping its own death. Preliminary to death is essentially discourse about death and thus its absence. What lends univocity shows itself to be equivocal.

Research has called attention to the equivocity of the use of concepts in

Being and Time, thereby implying that it is a matter of a lack of terminological precision that the author could have avoided.[3] Is it not more likely that the equivocity in the use of concepts is a vehicle for Heidegger's discourse, that it is the distinguishing characteristic of ontological analysis? This points to a realm in which opposites have not yet distanced themselves from each other. Insofar as such an analysis discusses simultaneously a precognitive totality and the normative opposites that issue from that totality, it must be equivocal. Such is the intention of chatter—in one moment, the always already given interpretation of the world, and in the next, the closing and concealment of that which actually is. Chatter is therefore ("before" all normative examination) the mediation of the human world through speech and at the same time (normative) that which distorts the passageway to authenticity.

If Heidegger wanted to introduce his concepts in a purely descriptive manner, he would have to abandon the assumption that supports everything ("alles tragende Vermutung") that man is not only a natural being but at the same time one also needed by others for the maintenance of the self and the securing of power (in his terminology, that being is simultaneously ontic and ontological). If he were to introduce the concepts in a purely normative fashion, he would be unable to develop the sphere of authenticity from an analysis of everyday existence. Heidegger thinks in asymmetrical polarities, whereby the negative pole (inauthenticity, chatter) contains the possibility of a positive counterpart (authenticity, "originally created" speech). Being there (Dasein) is "first and foremost" in inauthenticity, but as existence it also maintains the possibility of seizing or neglecting itself. In other words, the possibility is always given in the everyday to come to authenticity. In such reverse fashion from the authenticity disclosed in the prelude to death can the analysis of Dasein be performed.

But what does this have to do with equivocity? Are Heidegger's equivocal categories nonconcepts, or do they announce a new mode of thinking? Equivocity, in the negative sense of the word, is as such only for one who is in possession of univocity or intends to be. But if it seeks to establish human experience at its deepest levels as equivocal, then we must suspend, at the very least, the negative connotations associated with the word.

In the fragments to the *Passagenwerk,* Benjamin formulated the terrible thought that what we call progress might show itself as catastrophe. "That it 'so' continues" *is* the catastrophe."[4] The thought was endurable for Benjamin only because he saw the catastrophe that was unfolding before his eyes in the light of the messianic. The messiah arrives not as the redeemer but rather as the destroyer. The approach of the catastrophe is therefore always a sign of approaching redemption. That Benjamin, the materialist, makes use of theology is something he admits in one of the theses on history (he certainly leaves open whether things could stand otherwise and whether theology could make use of materialism). Heidegger severed the bridge with theology; he thinks the theological thought of salvation purely within the world. He does not seek, it is well noted, an equivalent within the realm of human endeavor for what theology calls redemption, but he will resituate theological thought in this world. That is only possible if he makes the theological view of the unity of catastrophe and redemption the basic form of his own thinking. It is only possible if he anticipates in thought the end of the world, in which all antinomies are collapsed, in order to think human history in terms of the prescribed end.

In Hölderlin's verse, "Wo aber Gefahr ist, wächst / Das Rettende auch" ("But where danger is, grows / the saving power also"),[5] a secret connection between danger and the savior is asserted. The words, nonetheless, are clearly separated from each other. In his interpretation, Heidegger intentionally goes beyond that: "The saving power is not secondary to danger. The selfsame danger is, when it is as the danger."[6] As danger, it is only insofar as it coincides with being: "Inasmuch as the danger is Being itself, it is both nowhere and everywhere. It has no place as something other than itself."[7]

We take care to encounter a danger that we can fathom; we seek to avoid a threatening event with precautionary measures. We imagine danger as something objectlike; we can oppose other objects to it. In short, equipped with the means of prescient calculation and technical trade, we deliver ourselves to danger. If, however, the danger in question stems from this posture toward the world (and Heidegger assumes it does), if it is how we stand in relation to the world that produces the danger, then certainly there can no longer be a place from which to undertake something against this danger. The danger is absolute; there is no outside. Even that which saves is necessarily a part of it.

The truth of the individual person is his death, the history of humanity's end—salvation and catastrophe—in one. Heidegger is thinking of an anticipated end. The end is also the end of all oppositions that the dialectic occupies in order, by way of those oppositions, to set the world in motion.

The dialectic as well recognizes death in various transformations: as the generative principle of life, as the result of the work of the understanding, and, finally, as the figure of the master. Steadfastly, the Hegelian master looks death in the face so as to disappear ultimately into it. He who would seek to stand over and against death must lend death his name (it is known that Hegel called death the "absolute master"). There is a reason for that, because the activity of the master revolves around death; he can only kill or die. Fear of death is a matter for the slave, who conquers it by serving the master. For the slave, it becomes something else, the stimulation of his abilities. He is the dialectician who sets the world in motion through the process of negation. In contrast, the master does not know any fear of death; that is, he already knows himself as the dead one who he will certainly become. A prelude to death is his action, through which oppositions are extinguished, oppositions that the slave experiences daily in objects. With an eye directed toward the end, the master stills the movement of the world and knows it to be vain.

It has often been asked why, following the war, Heidegger was not open about his engagement with National Socialism and did not admit his horrible error. Instead of seeking the reason in a character flaw in the person of the philosopher, attention was turned to his thinking. With relentless rigor, Heidegger thought through to the end the existence of the individual as well as the fate of humanity; from that perspective, there cannot be anything such as an error, for that presupposes normative oppositions as well as subjects that can understand them. The thinking of radical equivocity does not permit that. It knows life only in death.

10. Afterword

Inversions

Even the essay has its laws. Perhaps the strongest of these laws forbids it from taking stock, from pocketing its yield. Its movement of thought balks at any attempt, as one says, to get to the point. What, then, stirs the desire to write a conclusion? Is it a will to join texts to a whole, which in actuality they are not? Or is it anguish in the face of the irresponsible equivocity of the text? Anguish also perhaps that the odd thinking in which it is involved has taken over and now it would be effective, at the last moment, to help critique win its rights? Or is it simply the demand peculiar to theory in which a demand for mastery lurks? A distrust toward any will to synthesis might thus ensue, and not merely the bare renunciation of a conclusion that would betray the premises of the essay to relate experiences in unrelated fashion. Perhaps the essay can avoid being definitive by juxtaposing various results so that each disfigures the other and thereby restores inconclusiveness to the movement of thought.

Enfin Vint Kojève

From Bataille's persistent efforts to outdo Hegel to Roland Barthes's obvious lack of interest in his philosophy, it is not difficult to trace a tradition of French anti-Hegelianism. Like Bataille, Blanchot also wrestles with the colossus; the one by offering the contingency of pain in opposition to absolute knowledge ("A grand philosopher will only miss an aching tooth"); the other by performing, above all, Hegel's mode of thinking almost mimetically and thus committing to seek a site that might lie outside Hegelian thinking. Lacan, who is indebted to the *Phenomenology of Spirit* for many motifs in this thought, increasingly interprets his thought later as anti-Hegelianism. Belonging to a generation that had already distanced itself from Sartre, Foucault preserves from the outset a distance from Hegel and can bow more easily before Hegel and his French interpreter Hyppolite in his inaugural lecture at the Collège de France. To that, Roland Barthes had only to add in his autobiography a cynical pirouette: "And if I had never read Hegel [. . .]"[1]

In terms of the history of philosophy, anti-Hegelianism is easy to explain, whether as a continuation of French philosophy (rationalism, Enlightenment, positivism, neo-Kantianism) or as a reaction to the perceivable impact of Alexander Kojève's Hegel lectures of the 1930s. As plausible as either of the two explanations by itself might be, placing them next to each other calls them both into question. By contrast, the history of ideas might offer a remedy by combining both attempts at clarification. Against the backdrop of a tradition of thinking that holds itself aloof from the philosophy of German idealism, the Hegelianism represented by Kojève and Hyppolite remains an episode. . . .

Fatal for those explanations is that each easily awakens the appearance of plausibility, but none reaches to the impetus of the distancing from Hegel, which, since Bataille's 1937 letter to Kojève, has occupied French thinking. In his interpretation of the *Phenomenology,* Kojève had infused Hegel's philosophy existentially with a philosophy of death and, at the same time, politically with a philosophy of revolution. In subterranean fashion, he thus linked Heidegger and Marx to each other. The fascination of his lectures supposedly lay in this tension that lent listeners the impression of penetrating to the center of their own epoch. Precisely because Kojève's reading with Hegel presented history as virtually ended and Hegel's philosophy as insuperable knowledge, he provided the stimulus for thinking against this doubled end: that is, for working out with and against Hegel a philosophy of death.

Even if such an interpretation comes closer to the drama of the intellectual debate, it does not do justice to the fundamental thought. The discourse of anti-Hegelianism in French thinking is a construct that does not rise up to the reality of thought.

The Principle of Inversion

Experiences cannot be summarized. Indissolubly linked to the movement of the subject, they are representable solely as figures. They are infinitely different from each other as figures and resemble each other only in principle. But as we try to grasp the principle, the singularity of experience slips away.

With the exception of Roland Barthes (and this would require further investigation), all of the writers considered here are directly or indirectly related to surrealism. Even when they seek (like Bataille) to distance themselves from surrealism, agreement is recognizable behind the polemic. It suggests that the key for understanding the twentieth century is detectable in surrealism. The fascination that issues from it, and of which it is difficult to say whether it will begin to subside with the end of the century, stems from the fact that it is neither a literary-artistic movement nor a school of philosophy but rather, to speak with Blanchot, a *pratique d'existence,* "a praxis that yields its own knowledge, practical theory."[2]

One can perhaps express it quite simply: The surrealists rose up from their writing desks to find out whether it was still possible to have experiences. They thereby opened themselves to the problematic constellation that arrived with bourgeois society with the expressed intention to solve it, not through art or thinking but in reality. The constellation is the following: The bourgeois individual who presents himself as an autonomous, self-responsible subject experiences the society into which he was born as a world that inhibits everywhere his possibilities for actualization and that simultaneously is the result of human activity and thus his own activity. Where the solace of a better world beyond slips away, only art remains to close the gap and to reconcile the subject with the world. The symbolic artwork uniquely joins form and matter, subject and object, to a completed image at the cost of separating the sphere of art from the cultural battles of man and the world.

The surrealists are not satisfied with this solution. They scour reality for traces in which their desire might recognize itself again. Opposed to the facticity of estrangement, they posit the possibility of experience. But can one really make experience? Does language not lure us down a false path by persuading us of what we can "make"? The surrealists, in any case, regarded the turning away from productive work as the decisive requirement for experience. In a state of receptivity, one can be transported: Experience, however, is supposedly a matter of revelation. (Breton does not shy away from the concept *révélation,* although its religious connotations displease him.)

From the standpoint of the surrealists, bourgeois working existence functions to hinder experience. The first step of the surrealists, therefore, is preparation for idleness. In the emptiness created therewith, ennui breaks through, a weariness whereby everything is met with indifference. Surrealists expose themselves to it. Their protocols of experience (Aragon's *Paysan de Paris* and Breton's *Nadja*) offer reports of that. Ennui certainly has a counterpoint in the vague posture of expectation with which the flaneur roams the streets of the large city. Even if separated from each other, the extreme differences in mood, *attente,* and ennui coincide as conditions for embarking on surrealist experience. The world that the ennui turns away from indifferently is filled as well for the *attente* with indifferent (*gleichgültige*) things. This mere placing side by side suddenly brings for the surrealist self a thing, a pole of a still unapprehended attraction. Belated reflection first recognizes in it an image of desire. As if the wish had imagined itself in reality, subjectivity and objective givenness meet in unity. The moment in which that occurs, however, is the surrealist moment par excellence: every enduring sentiment abolished in the intoxication of fortune ("tout sentiment de durée aboli dans l'enivrement de la *chance*"[3]). The indifference of many things inverts itself in the (at first, only suspected) sensory fullness of the one, and the dullness of ennui or the indefiniteness of the *attente* takes on the firm outlines of concrete fortune. The found object stills specific longing, but at the same time, it contains the promise of a world in which subjective and objective orders prove themselves to be identical everywhere.

The surrealist compass for its odyssey through an urban landscape that has become a jungle is one of desire: not Hegelian desire (for desire's compass is not aimed at the negation of things but rather toward its symbolic pleasure). It seems instead to be closer to Lacanian desire (from which it is clearly distinguished by its knowledge of fulfillment): "individual motivating forces" by way of which the surrealist hopes for a different order of life.

Pratique d'existence, surrealism does not want to be literature; up until today, its explosive power has lain therein. It denies the independent scope of art, science, and politics in order to retrieve them as moments in the surrealist act that claims to be a moral-political deed, an aesthetic realization and a theory of its own act. The realization of the "true life" must always be deferred. "Existence is elsewhere." In any case, the surrealist has only fragments of an experience to report, that, were they whole, would be the true life. As something reported, they are subject to an inversion. The project targets experience that can only be related in reporting, which, as such, turns experience into something else: literature. This dilemma lends Breton's texts their particular suspense. The surrealist gesture is nonchalance. Breton's prose, however, has itself been recognized as the result of utmost effort. What do the texts say? Nonchalance or effort or both at the same time: Irrevocably, surrealism enters the realm of literature. Blanchot will pursue the question of what that means.

Perhaps this literary inversion actually comes to the aid of the surrealist project by preserving it from the possibility of its realization. That this can lead to a rude awakening is evident if one reads Tournier's *The Ogre* as a philosophical narrative that pursues the project to its final consequences. It suffices to remove innocence from desire, which is fitting under the light of surrealism. If its desire is ambivalent, if erotic and sadistic inclinations pervade that desire, then the dream of a concordance between the subjective and the objective world can find its fulfillment in the phantasm of the paranoid who experiences the fascist order as a realization of his wishes. The strategy of unsecuring, which the surrealists take up in the face of a rationally ordered world, is in this instance turned against its own project. This reveals that the complete sublation of alienation is closer to madness than the thinking in terms of definite oppositions ever anticipated.

In the middle of the 1930s, Bataille noted that his friends, who had come together around the publication *Acéphale,* had no respect for words, in contrast to the surrealists. Some shared condemnations of art and poesy originate from the same period. "Everything is false in the images of fantasy."[4] Strictly understood, each expression is a betrayal of what is to be expressed, of the first impulse in whose stead the sign enters. One would have to see in this the attempt to defend the existential project of surrealism against turning that project into literature. That also means restoring its intention to alter society. Unlike Breton, Bataille begins with the fundamental ambivalence of human wants. The principle of expenditure that occupies the center of his economic considerations is inseparable from the idea of catastrophe. Lust and horror coincide in ecstasy. Taking the place of surrealist *attente* is an activism that in the light of fascism calls out for an action, an action whose point of departure is literally unforseeable (*unabsehbar*).

The emphatic position of ambivalence blocks the process of experience, which requires stable oppositions. What in semiconscious mimesis drives him to his adversary, Bataille can no longer recognize as an inversion; he can only renounce it for the sake of turning to the strict solipsistic project of inner experience that confronts him anew with the dilemma of authentic expression. What Bataille calls "inner experience" is the will to experience what can no longer be experienced. Ecstatically, he seeks an equivalent for the impossible experience of death.

Bataille wants to rescue the existential project of surrealism, but he sets to it so profoundly that all concreteness burns out, that only the empty form of experience remains—ineffable ecstasy. Blanchot, by contrast, pursues inversions that occur in the moment when the project becomes literature.

The French Right also experienced an inversion of its will in the 1930s. What it regarded as strength it no longer found among its own people. As such, a Drieu La Rochelle found himself forced to prize it where he presumed to find it, "He who loves force, detects it, recognizes it everywhere it is. And if this force manifests itself against him, he must still take delight in it because of it. He must still take delight in mourning."[5] Drieu's way leads to collaboration. The decision produces a fact, for which he vouched at the end of the war with his death.

Can the existential project that is aimed at the entirety of existence continue without deadly consequences? Stated otherwise, can it return from the complete inversion of real action? Blanchot's answer to this question is paradoxical. The site of the project that goes all out is not the world of historical action but rather the world of literature. The self loses itself in language, which, by definition, is inversion. As the one writing, the self experiences that it cannot pronounce its own anguish but rather only the universal anguish in which its own disappears. Insofar as the self is delivered to language, it inverts its project and thus elides the inversion of action. As such, his own deed confronts the self as that of a stranger. The surrealist project of liberation becomes an auto-dafé in which the self is cremated in language.

Roland Barthes read Blanchot but also the literary critical essays of the early Sartre. Hegel and the surrealist project of "changer la vie" are removed from view, yet the later texts from Barthes read like a muted echo of the tensions present between wars. The will to authentic expression discovers the way to its fulfillment in the imitation of the outer bearing of recognized writers. The thought is the result of a rhetorical process; what appears as content to the reader is flashy exteriority: "as if I had a thought." The inversion is playful. Or is that mere deception? A conscious renunciation of the formulas of pathos?

With Lacan we entered the innermost circle of hell. Inversion is not the principle of experience that comes to us from the outside, nor is it the essence of language. Rather, it is a process that Lacan made use of. The entire deployment is transformed. Since the trauma of the rejection of his theory is turned into the guarantee of its truth, he turns his own self into the origin of truth. What language suggests to us holds for Lacan: He *makes* experiences. He thereby cuts himself off, we can presume, from what until now we have called experience. As the master of ambivalences, he is in charge of them: The self is simultaneously the site of necessary deception and absolute truth.

In the *Phenomenology of Spirit,* Hegel calls individuality the "principle of inversion." Individuality is the unsecured that posits this, then that, and can just as easily again sublate its own positing. For it, everything constantly turns into its opposite: the sought-after particular of unique pleasure in the abstract oneness of desire, which can be followed by a manifold, no less abstract. But it also holds for Hegel that the "movement of individuality is the reality of the universal" (*PG,* 291; *PS,* 229). Since the "way of the world is not as evil as it looked," the individuality that inverts everything cannot fall out of the rational whole. Its experience is far more retrievable in the world historical process than it is as a whole.

But what happens when the course of the world is as evil as it looks? All at once, the principle of inversion contains something that provokes anguish. No longer sublated, in spite of everything, in the rational totality of the world historical process, it constitutes that process as a succession of catastrophes. In the face of this, there are only a limited number of gestures: one can will them, suspend them in language, seek a playful engagement with them, or, finally, determine oneself as the knowledge of the catastrophe. These gestures describe limit experiences, all of which can be related to the forgotten figure of the bourgeois world, the figure of the master.

What Bataille calls sovereignty cannot simply be equated with the Hegelian master; the "whole man" nonetheless shares essential characteristics with Hegel's master, which is a refusal of productive activity and a readiness for death. It is not the derivation of a thinking (although Kojève's lectures on the idea of death in Hegel's philosophy might be offered as a means of connection) but rather a matter of its situating. Whereas Sartre in *Being and Nothingness* insists upon the contingency of human death and thus espouses the thinking of the slave, Bataille, Blanchot, and Lacan occupy the opposite position, for which Heidegger had offered the key phrase, "Being unto death." Lacan makes readiness for death a prerequisite of human freedom: "Man is starting with his death." And in Bataille, the will to a full life coincides with the readiness for self-abandonment.

The Thinking of the Master

In the chapter on lordship and bondage in the *Phenomenology of Spirit,* Hegel explains the origin of bourgeois society (if one understands origin in the Benjaminan sense, not as beginning but rather as underlying form). The battle for prestige results from a desire that appears human, since it does not seek something but rather the desire of another: the desire for recognition. If one excludes love as a path to this aim (and the realist Hegel does so), then only the battle unto life and death remains, the most hopeless of battles. For no matter how it turns out, neither of the combatants arrives at his goal. Dead, they cannot recognize each other. If one wins, the recognition is asymmetrical. The defeated may have saved his life, but he is not recognized. As slave, he works on things for the master out of fear of the master.

Whoever puts his life on the line and defeats the opponent is transformed into the master, who enjoys the fruits of the slave's labor. He is recognized, not by his own but rather by the slave, whom he himself did not recognize. The course of the tale is known. It tells of the slave's emancipation, who experiences resistance in the things on which he works out of fear of the master. That resistance permits him to come to himself. Hegel conceived the progression of the figures of consciousness on the basis of the slave, and Marx followed him in this respect by modeling the emancipation of the proletariat on that of the Hegelian slave.

Lordship is sublated by Hegel in the history of the slave. The anguish of death that the slave experiences and that forces him into submission and the fear of the master that constitutes his service are essential moments in the emancipation of the slave. Without fear of the master, the formative deed of the slave would be mere obstinacy, not work. The master is therefore necessary for Hegel's narrative. Without him there would be no history, but as history, he disappears from it. However one might interpret this disappearance—as the dialectically sequential sublation of lordship in the history of bourgeois emancipation or as the forgetting of lordship—it remains curious.

Certainly, sublation and forgetting are ways of disappearing in which what has disappeared remains. That holds as well for the figure of the master in the bourgeois world. The master is the shadow of the servant; he cannot get rid of him. Wherever the slave's project of emancipating comes upon a limit or is threatened by failure, that shadow is visible. Where history appears to be blocked, the gaze is directed to the figure of the master, who, looking death in the eye, stands aside from the bustle of history. Precisely because he promises no future, one reads in his features the fate of the present. If the logic of production leads to catastrophe without being able to think it, the logic of catastrophe appears as the truth of the epoch.

The existence of the master is the living critique of the slave's emancipation. The latter believes that he has conquered negativity by making it a master of endless productivity. But if progress reveals features of the catastrophic, can the thought not be far removed that negativity is not to be conquered but only repressed, that everything comes down to how one is positioned in relation to it? The thinking of the master does this. Certainly, the thinking of the master is not able to experience absolute negativity, that of his own death, but certainly he can experience its analog in ecstasy, in the disappearance of his own experience in language, and in the immediate positing of the errant one as truth. In each of these limit experiences, the self disappears in the act of self-realization. Where death is not grasped as a contingent occurrence but rather as an event according to which the self delineates itself, self-realization and self-dissolution coincide without mediation, as do all other dialectic oppositions that distinguish the thinking of the slave.

Whereas the slave who has come to self-consciousness knows his power, the master experiences his as a loss of consciousness. Whereas the slave carries over his productive activity onto history, which he regards as feasible, the master considers history to be a fate, which has ended before it has begun. In the restless doings of the slave, in which he surrounds himself with things, the master recognizes only the feigning of a real death.

The truth of the slave is knowledge of the might of the human act, of the figurability of the world, and of the realization of fortune. The truth of the master is knowledge of the loss of human consciousness, of the fatelike character of all history, and of the reality of death. Each truth places the other in question. The master regards the truth of the slave as blindness, the slave regards that of the master as backsliding into myth. Juxtaposing the effusive truth of the slave with the tragic one of the master, this thinking misses the configuration that forms both in relation to each other. For the thinking of the master denotes a limit experience that delimits the reason of the slave and to which it is attached. But where the thinking of the master grasps itself independently, its own truth is obscured for it.

The slave circulates in the world, posturing himself in technical fashion to it. But what in the end remains of his own doings are dead objects. The negativity of which he made use confronts him as something dead in which he cannot recognize his own activity. The dialectic, the great instrument of the slave, which should enable endless progress, strikes back at him. Incensed, he watches progress without being able to marshal it. The master stands to the side and smiles. He sees how the slave inverts history in fate and knows himself (the master) to be confirmed. He can do nothing with things. In contradistinction from the slave, for whom objects are things to be worked on, these objects are without determination for the master. He can only enjoy them, which, in the end, makes them threatening. He is even in discord with himself. In the deaths that he seeks, he does not die. The curse of repetition is inscribed in his activity. Repetition, however, "is the essence of the mystical occurrence."[6] Turning away from the myth of progress leads to the image of its opposite, which is no less mystical: the eternal return. Benjamin's archaeology of the nineteenth century has made that into the foundation of the modern. He could endure the thought of catastrophe because he viewed it in light of the messianic. For us, that light has gone out. Knowledge of death by the master does not lead out of the slavish logic of production; it is only its concealed backside.

Notes

Translator's Introduction

1. G. W. F. Hegel, *Phenomenology of Spirit,* trans. A. V. Miller (Oxford: Oxford University Press, 1977), 114 [hereafter cited in text as *PS* with page number]. Translations refer to but are not always consistent with Miller.

2. Bürger recounts Blanchot's own fond recalling of Levinas's notion of *autrui* in *The Infinite Conversation,* trans. Susan Hanson (Minneapolis: University Press of Minnesota, 1995).

3. Bürger does argue that the surrealist's disparaging characterization of Bataille as a librarian (*un 'assis' de bibliothèque*) is not unrelated to his thinking.

4. Bürger does try to justify this insertion of Heidegger, for example, into the Hegelian dialectic by relating it to Lacan's own appropriation of Heidegger's being unto death for his analysis of the master/slave dialectic.

5. Bürger repeatedly retreats from any assertion that the thinking of the master corresponds completely to the conditions of poststructuralist thought that he is outlining. Nonetheless, the shifts between consciousness and Being, for example, that enable his argument are not entirely confident ones.

6. See Walter Benjamin, "Goethes Wahlverwandtschaften," in *Illuminationen. Ausgewählten Schriften,* ed. Sigfried Unseld (Frankfurt am Main: Suhrkamp, 1977), 63–135.

7. Theodor Adorno, "On the Classicism of Goethe's *Iphigenie*" in *Notes to Literature,* vol. 2, trans. Sherry Webber Nicholsen (New York: Columbia University Press, 1992), 153–70. Bürger's faith in a restored dialectic might be stronger than I have portrayed. In exposing non-Hegelian thought to the dialectic, in bringing to consciousness its position as the "concealed backside" of the slave's consciousness, the effect might be for Bürger's thought to be absolutely Hegelian in its restoration to (self) consciousness of what had seemed to elide it.

Chapter I

1. Georg Lukács, *Die Seele und die Formen* (Neuwied and Berlin: Sammlung Luchterhand, 1971), 21.

2. Theodor W. Adorno, "Essay als Form," in *Noten zur Literatur,* vol. 1 (Frankfurt am Main: Suhrkamp, 1971), 16; Adorno, "The Essay as Form," in *Notes to Literature,* vol. 1, trans. Sherry Webber Nicholsen (New York: Columbia University Press, 1991), 23.

3. "Essay als Form," 29; "Essay as Form," 13.

4. Ibid.

Chapter 2

1. The English translation of the French, *Roi des Aulnes* (Paris: Gallimard, 1981), is *The Ogre,* trans. Barbara Bray (Baltimore: Johns Hopkins University, 1997) [hereafter cited in text as *RA* and *TO*]. The German title is *Der Erlkönig.* Thus the French and German titles retain reference to Goethe's famous poem.

2. Napola was the name given to Nazi paramilitary schools on the model of the famous imperial prytaneum at Ploen.—TRANSLATOR

3. André Breton, *Manifestes du surréalisme* (Paris: Gallimard, 23, 1963), 185 [hereafter cited in text as *MS*]. English translation refers to André Breton, *Manifestoes of Surrealism,* trans. Richard Seaver and Helen Lane (Ann Arbor: University of Michigan Press, 1969) [hereafter cited as *Eng.*].

4. Aragon certainly removed a few fragments from the auto-dafé during preprinting. They have recently been published as *La Défense de l'infini* (fragments), ed. E. Ruiz (Paris: Gallimard, 1986).

5. André Breton, *Nadja* (Paris: Gallimard, 1965), 20. The subsequent English translation is from André Breton, *Nadja,* trans. Richard Howard (New York: Grove, 1960), 19–20.

6. Jacques Lacan, *Ecrits* (Paris: Seuil, 1966), 170ff; G. W. F. Hegel, *Phänomenologie des Geistes,* ed. E. Moldenhauer and K. Michel, vol. 3 (Frankfurt am Main: Suhrkamp, 1973), 275ff [hereafter cited as *PG*].

The English refers to, but is not always consistent with, A. V. Miller's translation of Hegel's *Phänomenologie* (Oxford: Oxford University Press, 1977). As such, all translations of Hegel's text should be understood to be my own; page citations thus refer to the original German.—TRANSLATOR

7. See H. Ueberhorst, *Elite für die Diktatur* [. . .] (Düsseldorf: Droste, 1980), 90.

Chapter 3

1. Unless otherwise indicated, volume and page numbers refer to the following edition: George Bataille, *Oeuvres complètes,* 12 vols. (Paris: Gallimard, 1970–1973). Unless otherwise indicated, translations are from the French and are the translator's.

2. In the ironically entitled "Conclusion" to the *Archaeology of Knowledge,* Foucault made use of this figure of argumentation that renders the one speaking incomprehensible since he questions the possibility of his own speech.

3. On June 2, 1961, Bataille writes Kojève the following:

> I am no longer sure of still commanding some possibilities which once appeared to me . . . in particular, when it is about philosophy. Nevertheless, I want at least to attempt a sort of parallel to your *Introduction à la lecture Hegel,* but that

should be infinitely more arbitrary and founded principally on an effort to interpret what Hegel ignored, or neglected (thus, prehistory, the present, the future). It is not a matter of mocking the principle of the owl because it could be justified more than ever (as possibility, and perhaps as fatality, the final catastrophe) but to place at the very basis (or at the end) of Hegelian reflection an equivalence with madness: I would not know in truth how to specify what this is about—rather, what this will be about—until after having written it. But this sort of ending appears to me implied in the principle, if not of Hegelianism, then of its object.

George Bataille, *Lettres à Roger Caillois* [. . .], ed. J.-P. Le Bouler (Paris: Folle Avoine, 1987), 76.

4. M. Leiris, "De Bataille l'impossible à l'impossible 'Documents,' " in *Critique,* no. 195–96 (August-September 1963): 688.

5. "Surrealism intended to introduce not exactly into literary existence, considered as a specialized function, but into the whole of existence, a mode of activity that exceeded limits. Those limits were ones that fix not only laws but also customs and ones that enervate, in addition to thought and its expression, acts and attitudes." Bataille, in *La Critique sociale,* no. 7 (January 1933): 49.

6. See Michel Foucault, "Préface à la transgression," in *Critique,* no. 195–96 (August-September 1963): 751–69.

7. "I no longer wish to hold myself back from the errors of my fingers, from the errors of my eyes. I now know that these errors are not coarse traps but curious paths towards a goal that nothing else save these errors can show me. [. . .] New myths are born under every one of our steps," writes Aragon in the *Preface à une mythologie moderne,* the forward to *Paysan de Paris* (Paris: Gallimard, 1966), 15.

8. See D. Hollier, ed. *Le Collège de Sociologie (1937–39)* (Paris: Gallimard, 1979).

9. The previously published 1933 essay in *La Critique sociale,* edited by Boris Souvarine, forms the basis for the later study *La Part maudite* (1949).

10. George Bataille, *La Notion de dépense,* in *La Critique sociale,* no. 7 (January 1933): 7–15, here 9, 10.

11. George Bataille, *Lettres à Roger Caillois, 4 August 1935–4 February 1959,* ed. J.-P. Le Bouler (Paris: Folle Avoine, 1987), 93 [hereafter denoted as *LRC*]. That Bataille understands myth positively is evident from the lecture at the Collège, *L'Apprenti sorcier:* "Myth alone returns, to the one who is broken by every ordeal, the image of plenitude extended to the community where men gather" (1:535).

12. Boris Souvarine, prologue to the reprint of the periodical *La Critique sociale* (1931–34) (Paris: Editions de la Différence, 1983), 19.

13. "One would not know how to be clearer," writes, for example, the editor of the *Lettres à Roger Callois* in reference to the passage cited (*LRC,* 124n).

14. The following passage might shed some light on why I have chosen this formulation: "We see then [in fascism] rather a combination of interests: those of a

social class, those of a nation isolating itself, and those of a band of adventurers. It would have been otherwise had it been the expression of a philosophy, above all of a dramatic philosophy that spurred men of all sorts to life." (6:419).

15. "Time no longer belongs to clemency. Now in the world a great wind of subversion begins to blow, a cold wind, a stiff wind, an arctic one, one of those murderous and unhealthy winds that kill the delicate, the sick and the birds, a wind *that does not allow them to survive the winter*" (Roger Caillois, "Le Vent d'hiver," in Hollier, *Le Collège de Sociologie,* 96; emphasis in original).

16. Jean-Paul Sartre, *Un nouveau mystique* in *Situations I* [1947] (Paris: Gallimard, 1966), 187. Translation mine.—TRANSLATOR

17. Sartre, *Situations I,* 182.

18. Ibid., 156.

19. "So that man finally reveals himself to himself, he should die, but it would be necessary to do that while living—while watching himself cease to exist" (George Bataille, "Hegel, la mort et le sacrifice," in *Deucalon* 40 [October 1955]: 21–43, here 32.

Chapter 4

1. Maurice Blanchot, "De l'Angoisse à la littérature," in *Faux pas* [1943] (Paris: Gallimard, 1975) 9 [hereafter cited in text as *FP*]. English translation refers to Maurice Blanchot, *Faux Pas,* trans. Charlotte Mandel (Stanford, Calif.: Stanford University Press, 2001) [hereafter cited as *Eng.*].

2. Hegel, *PG,* 91; *PS,* 66.

3. Paul Valéry, *Cahiers,* vol. 2, ed. Judith Robinson (Paris: Gallimard, 1974), 1218.

4. Valéry's critique of Pascal, to which Blanchot is referring, is found in "Variation sur une pensée" (in *Oeuvres,* 2 vols., ed. J. Hytier [Paris: Gallimard, 1957, 1:458–73]). Blanchot offered a thorough discussion of Valéry's interpretation of Pascal in "La Main de Pascal" (in *La Part du feu* [1949] [Paris: Gallimard, 1972, 249–62]). Blanchot attempted to eliminate the dichotomy between romantic and antiromantic interpretations of Pascal.

5. In one respect Blanchot does, however, agree with Valéry; for both, solitude is the site of truth. "Alone,—that is to say, having for residence that which is and not that which appears—being the question and the response joined and not their division," Valéry writes in "Tel Quel," in *Oeuvres,* 2:536.

6. Søren Kierkegaard, *Philosophische Brosamen* [. . .], ed. H. Diem and W. Rest (Munich: dtv, 1976), 48f. Translation mine.—TRANSLATOR

7. Jean-Paul Sartre, "Présentation des Temps modernes," in *Situations II* [1948] (Paris: Gallimard, 1965), 9. Translation mine.—TRANSLATOR

8. Maurice Blanchot, *La Part du feu* [1949] (Paris: Gallimard, 1972), 33 [here-

after cited as *PF*]. English translation refers to Maurice Blanchot, *The Work of Fire,* trans. Charlotte Mandel (Stanford, Calif.: Stanford University Press, 1995), 26 [hereafter cited as *WF*].

9. Sartre, "Présentation," 13.

10. Maurice Blanchot, "La Parole vaine," in L. R. des Forêts, ed., *Le Bavard* (Paris: Union Générale d'Éditions, 1963), 179.

11. For Blanchot's relationship to Hegel, see Wanda Tommasi's reconstruction, "Per un' experienza non dialettica della parola. La presenza di Hegel nel primo Blanchot," in *Nuova Corrente* 32 (1985): 43–76. Also to F. Collin, *Maurice Blanchot et la question de l'écriture* (Paris: Gallimard, 1971). A. Warminski offers a reading inspired by Derrida, "Dreadful Reading: Blanchot on Hegel," in *Yale French Studies* 69 (1985): 267–75.

12. Blanchot places quotation marks around the sentence to suggest that he is relying upon a passage from the *Phenomenology of Spirit,* which, nonetheless, he clearly modifies in two ways, by translating "*ertragen*" (endure) as "*porter*" (*tragen* [carry]) and by relating it to language (*la parole*): "But the life of the Spirit is not the life that shrinks from death and keeps itself untouched by devastation, but rather the life that endures it and maintains itself in it" (Hegel, *PG,* 36; *PS,* 19).

13. Maurice Blanchot, *L'Entretien infini* [1969] (Paris: Gallimard, 1985), 85 [hereafter cited as *EI*]. English translation refers to Maurice Blanchot, *The Infinite Conversation,* trans. Susan Hanson (Minneapolis: University of Minnesota Press, 1993) [hereafter cited as *IC*].

14. Quoted in H. F. Fulda and D. Henrich, eds., *Materialien zu Hegels "Phänomenologie des Geistes"* (Frankfurt am Main: Suhrkamp, 1973), 154.

Chapter 5

This essay was first published in *Neue Rundschau* 101, no. 2 (1990): 113–14. The books of Barthes hereafter are cited in text and notes as follows:

CV—Critique et vérité (Paris: Seuil, 1966).

CT—Criticism and Truth, trans. Katrine Pilcher Keunemann (Minneapolis: University of Minnesota Press, 1987).

DZ—Le Degré zéro de l'écriture [1953] (Paris: Seuil, 1972).

WDZ—Writing Degree Zero, trans. Annette Lavers and Colin Smith (New York: Hill and Wang, 1968); English translation of *DZ.*

EC—Essais critiques [1964] (Paris: Seuil, 1981).

CE—Critical Essays, trans. Richard Howard (Evanston, Ill.: Northwestern University Press, 1972); English translation of *EC.*

EC4—Essais critiques IV: Le Bruissement de la langue (Paris: Seuil, 1984). Translation mine.—TRANSLATOR

M—Mythologies (Paris: Seuil, 1957).
Eng.—Mythologies, trans. Annette Lavers (London: Granada, 1980); English translation of *M.*
NEC—Nouveaux Essais critiques, in *DZ.*
NCE—New Critical Essays, trans. Richard Howard (New York: Hill and Wang, 1980); English translation of *NEC.*
RB—Roland Barthes (Paris: Seuil, 1975).
Eng.—Roland Barthes, trans. Richard Howard (New York: Hill and Wang, 1977); English translation of *RB.*
SFL—Sade, Fourier, Loyola [1971] (Paris: Seuil, 1980).
Eng.—Sade, Fourier, Loyola, trans. Richard Miller (New York: Hill and Wang, 1976); English translation of *SFL.*

1. In *Roland Barthes,* in which photographs assume the place of concrete experience, it says laconically in the commentary to a photograph of his two grandmothers, "the rest in Proust" (*RB,* 16).

2. Obviously, the English translation by Richard Miller differs from Barthes's actual text in this instance. "In the fashion" . . . "healthy" is deleted in the English. —TRANSLATOR

3. Gerard Genette has correctly pointed to that: "In Barthes signs are never neutral objects of a disinterested knowledge [. . .]. Normative choice is never too far behind analytical discourse" ("L'Envers des signes," in *Figures,* vol. 2 [Paris: Éditions du Seuil, 1966], 198). Translation mine.—TRANSLATOR

Chapter 6

This chapter was first presented in December 1988 at the Hamburg Foucault Conference and was first published in *Spiele der Wahrheit. Michel Foucaults Denken,* ed. F. Ewald and B. Waldenfels (Frankfurt am Main: Suhrkamp, 1991), 89–105. The lecturelike character of the text has been maintained.

Foucault's texts are denoted as follows:

AS—L'Archéologie du savoir [1969] (Paris: Gallimard, 1977).
AK—The Archaeology of Knowledge and the Discourse on Language, trans. A. M. Sheridan Smith (New York: Pantheon, 1972).
MC—Les Mots et les choses. Une archéologie des sciences humaines (Paris: Gallimard, 1966).
OT—The Order of Things (New York: Vintage, 1973).
OD—L'Ordre du discours [1971] (Paris: Gallimard, 1987).
"OD"—"The Order of Discourse," in *AK.*
"PT"—"Préface à la transgression," in *Critique,* no. 195–96 (August-September 1963): 751–69. Translation mine.—TRANSLATOR

SL—Schriften zur Literatur (Frankfurt: Ullstein, 1979).

UP—Histoire de la sexualité II: L'Usage des plaisirs (Paris: Gallimard, 1984).

HS—History of Sexuality II: The Use of Pleasure, trans. Robert Hurley (New York: Vintage, 1990).

1. H. Schnädelbach, "Morbus hermeneuticus, Thesen über eine philosophische Krankheit." In *Vernunft und Geschichte* [. . .] (Frankfurt am Main: Suhrkamp, 1987), 281.

2. Gilles Deleuze, *Foucault* (Paris: Minuit, 1986), 128. Translation mine. —TRANSLATOR

3. Ibid., 67.

4. See Foucault's essay "Was ist ein Autor?" in *SL,* 7–31.

5. Manfred Frank, *Was ist Neostrukturalismus?* (Frankfurt: Suhrkamp, 1983), 226. Translation mine.—TRANSLATOR

6. Ibid., 202.

7. Ibid., 242.

8. Jürgen Habermas, *Der philosophische Diskurs der Moderne* (Frankfurt: Suhrkamp, 1985), 316.

9. Pierre Bourdieu, *Leçon inaugurale faite le Vendredi 23 Avril 1982* (Paris: Collège de France, 1982).

10. He speaks of "meaning fluctuating around the word 'discourse' [. . .] sometimes it is the general domain of all statements, sometimes an individualizable group of statements, sometimes a regulated practice that accounts for a certain number of statements" (*AS,* 106; also see 141 and 153; *AK,* 80).

11. Georg Lukács, "Das Zerschellen der Form am Leben: Sören Kierkegaard und Regine Olsen," in *Die Seele und die Formen* [1911] (Neuwied: Sammlung Luchterhand, 1971), 44–63, here 44. Translation mine.—TRANSLATOR

12. Fichte uses the term in the *Wissenschaftslehre* to describe the self's positing of itself. There is no suitable English translation.—TRANSLATOR

13. Herein lies its proximity to Carl Schmitt's category of decision: "The decision frees itself from normative constraints and is, in a very real sense, absolute"; *Politische Theologie* [1922] (Berlin: Duncker and Humbolt, 1979), 19. Translation mine.—TRANSLATOR

14. "What, do you imagine that I would take so much trouble and pleasure [. . .], if I were not preparing—with a shaky hand—a labyrinth into which I can venture, in which I can move my discourse, opening up underground passages [. . .]," Foucault responds to his fictive critic, who has accused him of avoiding any sort of determination (*AS,* 28; *AK,* 17).

15. In his essay on Kierkegaard, Lukács works out the conditionality of the living gesture and thus its exposure to contradictory meanings as the opposing pole of its claim for absoluteness.

Chapter 7

1. Jacques Lacan, *Ecrits* (Paris: Éditions du Seuil, 1966), 193. English translation, when available, refers to Jacques Lacan, *Ecrits,* trans. Alan Sheridan (New York: W. W. Norton, 1977) [hereafter cited as *Eng.*]. Uncited English translations are the translator's.

2. Elsewhere, Miller translates this as "the heart of the matter" (G. W. F. Hegel, *Phenomenology of Spirit,* trans. A. Miller [Oxford: Oxford University Press, 1977], 246).—TRANSLATOR

Chapter 8

1. All page numbers refer to Jacques Derrida, *Glas* (Paris: Editions Galilée, 1974). English translation refers to Jacques Derrida, *Glas,* ed. John Leavey, Jr. and Richard Rand (Lincoln: University of Nebraska Press, 1990).

2. Derrida seeks to infer a shared basis of meaning—or, better, nonmeaning—from the phonetic similarities of the verbs.

Chapter 9

1. The following presentation is not a commentary on Heidegger's essay, "Nietzsches Wort 'Gott ist tot' " (in Martin Heidegger, *Holzwege* [Frankfurt: V. Klostermann, 1980], 205–64); it is much more an attempt to approach Heidegger's form of thinking without looking at a specific text.

2. In fact, we have tried to read Nietzsche's sentence with Heidegger's eyes. Nietzsche himself reads it otherwise. For him, the presence of the absent God is a menacing shadow that needs to be conquered. "After Buddha was dead, his shadow was still shown for centuries in a cave—a tremendous, gruesome shadow. God is dead; but given the way of men, there may still be caves for thousands of years in which his shadow will be shown.—And we—we still have to vanquish his shadow, too" (Friedrich Nietzsche, *The Gay Science,* trans. Walter Kaufmann [New York: Vintage, 1974]), n. 108.

3. Barbara Merker, *Selbstäuschung und Selbsterkenntnis. Zu Heideggers Transformation der Phänomenologie Husserls* (Frankfurt am Main: Suhrkamp, 1998), 124, 219.

4. Walter Benjamin, *Gesammelte Schriften,* vol. 5, ed. R. Tiedemann (Frankfurt: Suhrkamp, 1982), 592. Translation mine.—TRANSLATOR

5. Martin Heidegger, "Die Kehre," in *Die Technik und die Kehre* (Pfullingen: Neske, 1982), 41. English translation from Martin Heidegger, "The Turning," in

The Question Concerning Technology and Other Essays, trans. William Lovitt (New York: Harper and Row, 1977), 36–52; here 42.

6. Heidegger, "The Turning," 42.

7. Ibid., 43.

Chapter 10

1. Roland Barthes, *Roland Barthes,* trans. Richard Howard (New York: Hill and Wang, 1977), 100.

2. Maurice Blanchot, *L'Entretien infini* [1969] (Paris: Gallimard, 1986), 597.

3. André Breton, *L'Amour fou* [1937] (Paris: Gallimard, 1976), 38.

4. George Bataille, *Oeuvres complètes,* vol. 1 (Paris: Gallimard, 1970), 526.

5. P. Drieu La Rochelle, "Entre l'hiver et le printemps" [1942] in *Sur les Écrivains,* ed F. Grover (Paris: Gallimard, 1982), 160.

6. Walter Benjamin, *Gesammelte Schriften,* vol. 5, ed R. Tiedemann (Frankfurt: Suhrkamp, 1982), 178. Translation mine.—TRANSLATOR

Works Cited

Adorno, Theodor W. "Essay als Form." In *Noten zur Literatur.* Vol. 1. Frankfurt am Main: Suhrkamp, 1971.

———. "The Essay as Form." In *Notes to Literature.* Vol. 1. Trans. Sherry Webber Nicholsen. New York: Columbia University Press, 1991.

———. "On the Classicism of Goethe's *Iphigenie.*" In *Notes to Literature.* Vol. 2. Trans. Sherry Webber Nicholsen. New York: Columbia University Press, 1992.

Aragon. *La Défense de l'infini* (fragments). Ed. E. Ruiz. Paris: Gallimard, 1986.

———. *Paysan de Paris.* Paris: Gallimard, 1966.

Barthes, Roland. *Critical Essays.* Trans. Richard Howard. Evanston, Ill.: Northwestern University Press, 1972.

———. *Criticism and Truth.* Trans. Katrine Pilcher Keunemann. Minneapolis: University of Minnesota Press, 1987.

———. *Critique et vérité.* Paris: Seuil, 1966.

———. *Essais critiques.* Paris: Seuil, 1972.

———. *Essais critiques IV: Le Bruissement de la langue.* Paris: Seuil, 1984.

———. *Le Degré zéro de l'écriture.* Paris: Seuil, 1972.

———. "L'Exclusion." *Neue Rundschau* 101, no. 2 (1990): 113–14.

———. *Mythologies.* Paris: Seuil, 1957.

———. *Mythologies.* Trans. Annette Lavers. London: Granada, 1980.

———. *New Critical Essays.* Trans. Richard Howard. New York: Hill and Wang, 1980.

———. "*Nouveaux Essais critiques*" ("Suive de Nouveaux essais critiques"). In *Le Degré zéro de l'écriture.* Paris: Seuil, 1972.

———. *Roland Barthes.* Paris: Seuil, 1975.

———. *Roland Barthes.* Trans. Richard Howard. New York: Hill and Wang, 1977.

———. *Sade, Fourier, Loyola.* Paris: Seuil, 1980.

———. *Sade, Fourier, Loyola.* Trans. Richard Miller. New York: Hill and Wang, 1976.

———. *Writing Degree Zero.* Trans. Annette Lavers and Colin Smith. New York: Hill and Wang, 1968.

Bataille, Georges. "Hegel, la mort et le sacrifice." In *Deucalon* 40 (October 1955): 21–43.

———. "La Notion de dépense." *La Critique sociale,* no. 7 (January 1933): 7–15.

———. *La Part Maudit. Essai d'èconomie gènèrale.* Paris: Minuit, 1949.

———. *Lettres à Roger Callois, 4 août 1935–4 fevrier 1959.* Ed. J.-P. Le Bouler. Paris: Folle Avoine, 1987.

———. *L'Expérience intérieure.* Paris: Gallimard, 1954.

———. *Oeuvres complètes.* 12 vols. Paris: Gallimard, 1970–73.

Benjamin, Walter. *Gesammelte Schriften.* Vol. 5. Ed. R. Tiedemann. Frankfurt am Main: Suhrkamp, 1982.

———. "Goethes Wahlverwandtschaften." In *Illuminationen. Ausgewählten Schriften.* Ed. Siegfried Unseld. Frankfurt am Main: Suhrkamp, 1977.

Blanchot, Maurice. *Faux pas.* Paris: Gallimard, 1975.

———. *Faux Pas.* Trans. Charlotte Mandel. Stanford, Calif.: Stanford University Press, 2001.

———. "La Parole vaine." In *Le Bavard.* Ed. L. R. de Forêts. Paris: Union Générale d'Éditions, 1963.

———. *La Part du feu.* Paris: Gallimard, 1972.

———. *L'Entretien infini.* Paris: Gallimard, 1986.

———. *The Infinite Conversation.* Trans. Susan Hanson. Minneapolis: University of Minnesota Press, 1993.

———. *The Work of Fire.* Trans. Charlotte Mandel. Stanford, Calif.: Stanford University Press, 1995.

Bourdieu, Pierre. *Leçon inaugurale faite le Vendredi 23 Avril 1982.* Paris: Collège de France, 1982.

Breton, Andre. *L'Amour fou.* Paris: Gallimard, 1976.

———. *Manifestes du surréalisme.* Paris: Gallimard, 1963.

———. *Manifestoes of Surrealism.* Trans. Richard Seaver and Helen Lane. Ann Arbor: University of Michigan Press, 1969.

———. *Nadja.* Paris: Gallimard, 1965.

———. *Nadja.* Trans. Richard Howard. New York: Grove, 1960.

Collin, Françoise. *Maurice Blanchot et la question de l'écriture.* Paris: Gallimard, 1971.

Deleuze, Gilles. *Foucault.* Paris: Minuit, 1986.

Derrida, Jacques. *Glas.* Paris: Galilée, 1974.

———. *Glas.* Trans. John Leavey Jr. and Richard Rand. Lincoln: University of Nebraska Press, 1990.

Drieu La Rochelle, Pierre. "Entre l'hiver et le printemps." In *Sur les Écrivains.* Ed. F. Grover. Paris: Gallimard, 1982.

Ewald, F., and B. Waldenfels, eds. *Spiele der Wahrheit. Michel Foucaults Denken.* Frankfurt am Main: Suhrkamp, 1991.

Fichte, Johann Gottlieb. *Wissentschaftslehre.* Trans. George Seidel. West Lafayette, Ind.: Purdue University Press, 1993.

Foucault, Michel. *Histoire de la sexualité.* Vol. 2, *L'Usage des plaisirs.* Paris: Gallimard, 1984.

———. *History of Sexuality.* Vol. 2, *The Use of Pleasure.* Trans. Robert Hurley. New York: Vintage, 1990.

———. *L'Archéologie du savoir.* Paris: Gallimard, 1977.

———. *Les Mots et les choses. Une archéologie des sciences humaines.* Paris: Gallimard, 1966.

———. *L'Ordre du discours.* Paris: Gallimard, 1986.

———. "Préface à la transgression." *Critique,* no. 195–96 (August-September 1963): 751–69.

———. *Schriften zur Literatur.* Frankfurt: Ullstein, 1979.

———. *The Archaeology of Knowledge and the Discourse on Language.* Trans. A. M. Sheridan Smith. New York: Pantheon, 1972.

———. *The Order of Things.* New York: Vintage, 1973.

Frank, Manfred. *Was ist Neostrukturalismus?* Frankfurt am Main: Suhrkamp, 1983.

Fulda, H. F., and D. Henrich, eds. *Materialien zu Hegels "Phänomenologie des Geistes."* Frankfurt am Main: Suhrkamp, 1973.

Genette, Gerard. "L'Envers des signes." In *Figures.* Vol. 2. Paris: Seuil, 1966.

Habermas, Jürgen. *Der philosophische Diskurs der Moderne.* Frankfurt am Main: Suhrkamp, 1985.

Hegel, Georg Wilhelm Friedrich. *Phänomenologie des Geistes.* Vol. 3. Eds. E. Moldenhauer and K. Michel. Frankfurt am Main: Suhrkamp, 1973.

———. *Phenomenology of Spirit.* Trans. A. V. Miller. Oxford: Oxford University Press, 1977.

Heidegger, Martin. "Die Kehre." In *Die Technik und die Kehre.* Pfullingen: Neske, 1982.

———. "Nietzsches Wort 'Gott ist tot.'" In *Holzwege.* Frankfurt am Main: V. Klostermann, 1980.

———. "The Turning." In *The Question Concerning Technology and Other Essays.* Trans. William Lovitt. New York: Harper and Row, 1977.

Hollier, D., ed. *Le Collège de Sociologie. Textes de George Bataille 1937–39.* Paris: Gallimard, 1979.

Kierkegaard, Søren. *Philosophische Brosamen und Unwissenschaftliche Nachscrift.* Ed. H. Diem and W. Rest. Munich: dtv, 1976.

Lacan, Jacques. *Ecrits.* Paris: Seuil, 1966.

———. *Ecrits.* Trans. Alan Sheridan. New York: W. W. Norton, 1977.

Leiris, M. "De Bataille l'impossible à l'impossible 'Documents.'" *Critique,* no. 195–96 (August-September 1963): 688.

Lukács, Georg. *Die Seele und die Formen.* Neuwied: Luchterhand, 1971.

Merker, Barbara. *Selbstäuschung und Selbsterkenntnis. Zu Heideggers Transformation der Phänomenologie Husserls.* Frankfurt am Main: Suhrkamp, 1998.

Nietzsche, Friedrich. *The Gay Science.* Trans. Walter Kaufmann. New York: Vintage, 1974.

Sartre, Jean-Paul. *Situations.* Vols. 1–2. Paris: Gallimard, 1966.

Schmitt, Carl. *Politische Theologie.* Berlin: Duncker and Humbolt, 1979.

Schnädelbach, Herbert. "Morbus hermeneuticus. Thesen über eine philosophische Krankheit." In *Vernuft und Geschichte.* Frankfurt am Main: Suhrkamp, 1987.

Souvarine, Boris. Prologue to reprint of *La Critique Sociale* (1931–1934). Paris: Différence, 1983.

Tommasi, Wanda. "Per un' esperienza non dialettica della parola. La presenza di Hegel nel primo Blanchot." *Nuova Corrente,* no. 32 (1985): 43–76.

Tournier, Michel. *Le Roi de Aulnes.* Paris: Gallimard, 1981.

———. *The Ogre.* Trans. Barbara Bray. Baltimore: Johns Hopkins University Press, 1981.

Ueberhorst, Horst. *Elite für die Diktatur; die Nationalistischen Erziehungsanstalten 1933–1945.* Düsseldorf: Droste, 1945.

Valéry, Paul. *Cahiers.* Vol. 2. Ed. Judith Robinson. Paris: Gallimard, 1974.

———. *Oeuvres.* Vol. 2. Ed. J. Hytier. Paris: Gallimard, 1957–1960.

Warminski, Andrzej. "Dreadful Reading: Blanchot on Hegel." *Yale French Studies,* no. 69 (1985): 267–75.

Peter Bürger is the author of *Theory of the Avant-Garde* and *The Decline of Modernism* and coauthor, with Christa Bürger, of *The Institutions of Art*. Until his retirement, he was a professor of Romance studies at the University of Bremen.

Richard Block is an assistant professor in the Department of Germanic and Slavic Languages and Literatures at the University of Colorado at Boulder.